Transport and the
State of Trade in Britain

THOR HULTGREN

Assisted by
WILLIAM I. GREENWALD

OCCASIONAL PAPER 40

NATIONAL BUREAU OF ECONCMIC RESEARCH, INC.

Transport and the
State of Trade in Britain

THOR HULTGREN

Assisted by

WILLIAM I. GREENWALD

OCCASIONAL PAPER 40

NATIONAL BUREAU OF ECONOMIC RESEARCH, INC.

1953

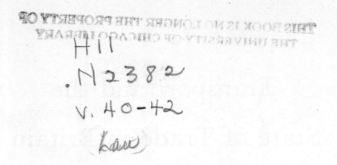
Typography by Oscar Leventhal, Inc.
Printing by John N. Jacobson & Son, Inc.

Library of Congress catalog card number: 54-6460

PRICE: $1.50

Relation of the Directors
to the Work and Publications
of the National Bureau of Economic Research

1. The object of the National Bureau of Economic Research is to ascertain and to present to the public important economic facts and their interpretation in a scientific and impartial manner. The Board of Directors is charged with the responsibility of ensuring that the work of the National Bureau is carried on in strict conformity with this object.

2. To this end the Board of Directors shall appoint one or more Directors of Research.

3. The Director or Directors of Research shall submit to the members of the Board, or to its Executive Committee, for their formal adoption, all specific proposals concerning researches to be instituted.

4. No report shall be published until the Director or Directors of Research shall have submitted to the Board a summary drawing attention to the character of the data and their utilization in the report, the nature and treatment of the problems involved, the main conclusions and such other information as in their opinion would serve to determine the suitability of the report for publication in accordance with the principles of the National Bureau.

5. A copy of any manuscript proposed for publication shall also be submitted to each member of the Board. For each manuscript to be so submitted a special committee shall be appointed by the President, or at his designation by the Executive Director, consisting of three Directors selected as nearly as may be one from each general division of the Board. The names of the special manuscript committee shall be stated to each Director when the summary and report described in paragraph (4) are sent to him. It shall be the duty of each member of the committee to read the manuscript. If each member of the special committee signifies his approval within thirty days, the manuscript may be published. If each member of the special committee has not signified his approval within thirty days of the transmittal of the report and manuscript, the Director of Research shall then notify each member of the Board, requesting approval or disapproval of publication, and thirty additional days shall be granted for this purpose. The manuscript shall then not be published unless at least a majority of the entire Board and a two-thirds majority of those members of the Board who shall have voted on the proposal within the time fixed for the receipt of votes on the publication proposed shall have approved.

6. No manuscript may be published, though approved by each member of the special committee, until forty-five days have elapsed from the transmittal of the summary and report. The interval is allowed for the receipt of any memorandum of dissent or reservation, together with a brief statement of his reasons, that any member may wish to express; and such memorandum of dissent or reservation shall be published with the manuscript if he so desires. Publication does not, however, imply that each member of the Board has read the manuscript, or that either members of the Board in general, or of the special committee, have passed upon its validity in every detail.

7. A copy of this resolution shall, unless otherwise determined by the Board, be printed in each copy of every National Bureau book.

(Resolution adopted October 25, 1926 and revised February 6, 1933 and February 24, 1941)

Contents

Foreword

In the concluding chapter of *American Transportation in Prosperity and Depression*[1] Mr. Hultgren set forth the implications of his study for future cycles. If cycles in general business should continue to occur, how would railway, highway, and air traffic react? What changes in the rate of utilization of equipment would take place? How would the productivity of labor in the industry be affected? What changes in costs and profits might be expected? The present paper provides a test of some of Hultgren's answers to these questions — a test based not upon subsequent cycles in the United States, but upon the cyclical behavior of transportation services in another country, Great Britain. Like the previous study, it is devoted largely, though not exclusively, to railway transportation and contains data bearing on secular as well as cyclical developments.

The general course of development of the railroad industry in the United States has been similar in many respects to that in Britain. Railroad construction, of course, began first in England. By 1870, however, the tonnage of freight handled by railroads in the United States began to surpass that handled by railroads in Britain, and the rate of growth in the United States has exceeded that in Britain decade by decade with one significant exception: the decade of the thirties. The number of passengers carried by railroads, on the other hand, has always been considerably larger in Britain, despite its smaller population, and in passenger traffic the percentage rates of growth in the two countries have been more alike than in freight traffic. However, the rates of growth in both types of traffic in both countries have declined rather steadily with the passage of time, exhibiting the retardation so characteristic of the growth of individual industries.

One of the factors contributing to this retardation, especially after

[1] (National Bureau of Economic Research, 1948.)

World War I, was the competition from highway transport. The pressure was particularly severe on railway passenger traffic, as the following percentage changes, 1920-48, indicate. Although railroad freight traffic advanced during this interval, in neither country did it keep pace with industrial production.

	United States	Great Britain
	(per cent change)	
Number of passengers	−49	−42
Freight ton-miles	+55	+12
Industrial production	+156	+57

In *American Transportation in Prosperity and Depression* Hultgren made the interesting observation that the diversion of freight traffic from railroads to other transportation agencies took place more rapidly during general business contractions than during business expansions. He now reports a similar result for Britain. Apparently in both countries cyclical contractions have stimulated the shift from rail to truck transport, whether because contraction induces shippers to seek lower costs more energetically or because trucking rates and costs are more flexible in the cycle.

Despite this competitive pressure, which had a similar effect on traffic trends in both countries, it appears that the technological development of British railways has not kept pace with American roads. For example, Hultgren's charts show that during the interwar period the average speed of freight trains rose considerably in the United States, but was virtually constant in Britain. Similarly, traffic per ton of fuel consumed rose in the United States, but stood still in Britain. These differences evidently reflect more rapid adoption of improved equipment by railroads in this country. The net result, to which other factors have also contributed, has been that the amount of labor required per unit of traffic volume is far smaller in the United States than in Britain, and the decline in this requirement in the past thirty years has been far greater in this country. For example, in 1948 railways in the United States carried nearly thirty times as much freight traffic (ton-miles) and nearly twice as much passenger traffic (passenger-miles) as British railways, yet they employed only twice as many men.

Because the present study, like Hultgren's earlier investigation, is focused largely upon the cyclical behavior of costs, the factors affecting costs, and the resulting effects on profits, its significance reaches beyond the transportation industry. The behavior of costs and profits is basic to our understanding of business cycles, and the voluminous data available for the transportation industry make it a useful testing ground for theories concerning such behavior. As the reader will discover from Hultgren's carefully documented account, summed up in Section 8, the behavior typical of American railroads is also typical, in the main, of British railroads.

For example, he finds that the stock of railway equipment bears no consistent relationship to cyclical variations in railroad traffic or general business activity. True, additions to stock are generally higher in years of high than in years of low activity. Yet in the shorter cycles these additions often behave counter-cyclically, and even in the longer contractions net additions often continue to be made, so that there is no decline in the stock. This seems to be as true for Britain as for the United States.

The present study also supports Hultgren's previous finding that "variable costs" per unit of traffic are inversely related to the volume of traffic. In physical terms, the volume of labor, fuel, or purchased materials does not ordinarily rise or fall in proportion to traffic. Moreover, although prices of these factors tend to rise and fall with railroad traffic and with general business activity, the variations are usually not sufficient to offset the opposite changes in unit physical costs. This, together with a high degree of stability in the prices of railway services, leads to the result that a cyclical expansion in traffic has usually been accompanied by a rise not only in aggregate profits but also a rise in profits per unit of traffic, whereas a contraction brings with it a decline in unit profits as well as aggregate profits.

What is true of the railroad industry is not necessarily true of other industries. The influence of volume of business on unit costs must obviously vary widely from one industry to another, and so must the relative changes in factor prices and finished product prices. Unfortunately, detailed factual studies of the kind Hultgren has made are all too rare. But the patient accumulation of systematic bodies of evidence of this sort is the only way to achieve a secure understanding of the processes that generate business cycles.

GEOFFREY H. MOORE

Acknowledgments

Vera Wantman Kopelman and Johanna Stern patiently and energetically helped assemble the statistics and general information for this paper.

Among the directors and personnel of the National Bureau, Harold Barger, Arthur F. Burns, Louise Cooper, G. A. Elliott, Frank W. Fetter, Millard Hastay, Ruth P. Mack, Geoffrey H. Moore, C. Reinold Noyes, and Harold F. Williamson read manuscript versions of the paper and suggested various improvements in style and substance. C. E. R. Sherrington and E. A. Toneri of the Railway Research Service in London examined a preliminary draft, and the final product has benefitted from their wide acquaintance with the economics and technique of transport as well as their proximity to the British scene. A. W. Currie of the University of Toronto sent me informed and useful comments.

H. Irving Forman's fine draftsmanship is evident in the charts.

The extensive collection of British documents in the Economics Division of the New York Public Library was of great assistance. The New York offices of the British Library of Information and of British and Irish Railways, Inc., were courteously helpful.

Thor Hultgren

Introductory: Traffic and Business

After many decades of industrialization, Britain still has fields and barns, and they continue to give forth crops and livestock. Men still cut timber in the shrunken forests. Great tonnages of goods emerge from mines and factories. Fish are landed from the environing sea, and imports come across it. The yield of all these sources combined may be called the flow of commodities. There are no long-run statistical measures of this grand composite, but if there were they would no doubt show it increasing at some times and diminishing at others, in waves like those we have in mind when we speak of business cycles. The transport enterprises in Britain participate in this flow, and their goods traffic is likely to rise and fall in similar cycles. Associated with these fluctuations, there must be changes in the occasions for business travel and the amounts people feel they can afford to spend for social and pleasure travel. The fluctuations in traffic affect in turn the economy and profitability of transport enterprises.

The variations in the aggregate flow of commodities must have paralleled in a general way the cycles that Burns and Mitchell have chronicled in British business activity at large. In this paper we shall investigate the relation between changes in traffic and the cycles in total business, which Burns and Mitchell call "reference" cycles. In the process we shall find cycles in traffic itself; later we shall trace the effect of these traffic cycles on other aspects of transport operations, including their cost and profitability.

We can observe these interrelations chiefly in the working of railways; the statistical record of other transport enterprises is less abundant. Even the record for railways, through 1913, is confined to annual data on the more salient aspects of their operations. No statistics were published for the war years 1914-18. Beginning in 1920 or later, ending temporarily in the middle of 1939, and resuming in 1944, there are

1

monthly or quarterly figures on many aspects of operation; for the study of cycles they are preferable to annual figures, and we shall use them whenever possible. Because of these breaks in the data, the various charts and tables we present necessarily cover varying periods of time.

The responses of transport officials and employees to fluctuations in traffic and earnings have repercussions on the rest of the economy; thus they are one of the many interwoven aspects of business cycles. Other aspects have been or will be described by various investigators in the course of the National Bureau's comprehensive inquiry into business disturbances. The transportation studies have been planned as a part of that inquiry.[1]

---

[1] A different approach may be found in C. Douglas Campbell's *British Railways in Boom and Depression* (P. S. King, London, 1932). Campbell fitted trend lines to annual data on the percentage of workers employed in industry, 1878-1912, and to data for the same period on various aspects of railway activity — goods carried, passengers, revenues, expenses, train miles, etc. He computed the year-by-year deviations from each trend, found cycles in the deviations, and made comparisons among the various kinds of data with respect to the timing and amplitude of their deviation cycles. This method was not applied to later periods; for the postwar years, Campbell felt that a comparison with prewar levels, and an analysis of the rate-making provisions in the Railways Act, 1921, from a cyclical point of view, would be more pertinent and illuminating.

1. The Movement of Goods

Traffic was intimately related to production of coal

Although we have no measure of the grand composite flow of all commodities we do have a measure of the flow, from its origin in the ground, of the commodity which, in raw or simply manufactured form, is the most important single source of traffic. After World War I, coal, coke, and the so-called patent fuel (the raw material and the two products are lumped together in the traffic statistics) accounted for considerably more than half of the total tonnage originated by the railways, and for about half of the total movement of goods (measured in ton-miles). Doubtless coal and related traffic was comparably important in earlier periods. The total flow of coal and its products is roughly measured by the statistics of coal production. Although coal traffic was not separately reported before the war, the great bulk of the "minerals conveyed" must have been coal. The relation between total flow of coal and railway traffic was close. For every cyclical wave in coal production, as far as we can tell from the prewar data, there was a corresponding cycle in mineral traffic (Chart 1). Whenever the mine operators increased their output from one year to the next, the railway companies enjoyed an increase in their minerals traffic. Whenever output diminished, the traffic diminished. Minor exceptions to these general observations occurred in 1856-58, 1884-85, and 1897-98. The very slight decline in production from 1919 to 1920 was accompanied by a slight increase in tonnage originated, but the sharper decline in output from 1920 to 1921 was accompanied by a sharp decline in tonnage (Table 1).

Statistics of ton-miles reflect not only the weight of shipments but the length of movement. They therefore measure freight traffic more comprehensively than statistics of tons originated or conveyed measure it. Ton-mile data were first collected for 1920. From that year to 1938

3

every cycle in production was accompanied by a cycle in coal and coal product ton-miles (Chart 2).[1]

Traffic cycles corresponded to trade cycles

In a looser and more general way, cycles in total traffic can be matched with the cycles that occurred, according to Burns-Mitchell, in general business activity. From 1857 to 1913, the railways carried more ton-

TABLE 1
Coal Production
Rail Tonnage Originated, by Kind, 1919-1921
(millions of tons)

| | COAL PRODUCTION | TONS ORIGINATED[a] | | | |
		General merchandise	Coal, coke, and patent fuel	Other minerals	Total
1919	229.8	68.4	180.1	56.4	304.9
1920	229.5	68.7	181.2	68.1	318.1
1921	163.3	50.5	128.3	39.1	217.9

[a] See note to Table 2.

nage in each[2] year of every business expansion than they did in the preceding year (Chart 1, top line). Traffic diminished from year to year throughout 3 of the 9 contractions. It diminished part of the time in 4 others. In the remaining 2 it increased, but the average annual gain was smaller in each case than in the immediately neighboring expansions. Indeed in every general business contraction the annual average change was either a fall or a smaller rise than in the preceding or following phase (Table 2). Total tonnage originated rose in the 1919-20 business expansion and fell in the 1920-21 contraction (Table 1). There was a cycle in total ton-miles for every business cycle from 1920 to 1938 (Chart 3).

[1] Annual coal production from Richard Meade, *Coal and Iron Industries of the United Kingdom* (C. Lockwood & Co., London, 1882), p. 296, through 1872, and from Secretary of Mines, *Annual Report,* thereafter. For source of monthly data, see Table 7, note a.

As in later charts and tables, the monthly data are seasonally adjusted. Cf. note on sources.

In this and other charts, asterisks mark peaks and troughs in the economic activities charted.

[2] With one exception: from 1911 to 1912 there was a slight dip, followed by a vigorous rise to 1913, the closing year of the reference expansion. A coal strike from February 26 to April 15, 1912 explains this exception. There was no dip in general merchandise conveyed.

4

CHART 1

Tons Conveyed by Railways
Total, 1856-1868, 1871-1913
Minerals, General Merchandise, 1856-1868, 1872-1902, 1903-1913
Coal Production, 1856-1916

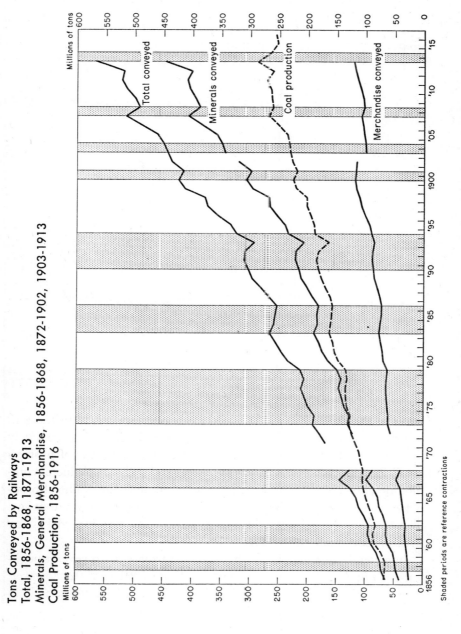

Shaded periods are reference contractions

CHART **2**

Coal: Production and Movement by Rail
January 1920-April 1939

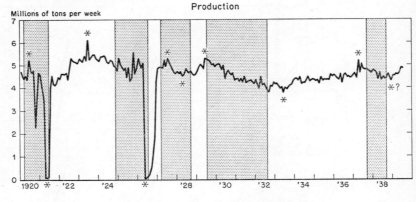

Production

Millions of tons per week

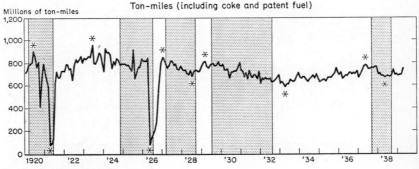

Ton-miles (including coke and patent fuel)

Millions of ton-miles

Shaded periods are reference contractions.

Since the cycles in total traffic corresponded so closely to those in minerals or coal traffic, there would be no point in discussing separately the relation of the latter to the trade cycle. For the study of business conditions, moreover, the figures for merchandise, i.e. nonmineral commodities, are of greater interest. In terms of employment, value of product, etc., coal is not as important as it is in terms of railway tonnage. The revenue the railways themselves receive for carrying coal is less than proportionate to the tons carried.

In general, merchandise traffic increased from year to year throughout each business expansion (Chart 1). From 1901 to 1902, however, it fell slightly.[3] There were declines in traffic corresponding exactly in

[3] There are no figures for 1869 or 1870; the figure for 1871 is not comparable with that for other years, and that for 1903 is not comparable with 1902 or earlier years.

TABLE **2**

Tons of Freight Conveyed

Change per Year between Peak and Trough in Business, 1857-1913

REFERENCE DATE	LEVEL OF BUSINESS	TONS CONVEYED (MILLIONS)[a]	PERCENTAGE CHANGE		ABSOLUTE CHANGE		ABSOLUTE CHANGE PER YEAR	
			To peak from preceding trough	To trough from preceding peak	Millions of tons	Years elapsed	To peak from trough	To trough from peak
1857	Peak	71.3	.....	.....	.....	.....	.....	.....
1858	Trough	73.1	.....	2.52	1.8	1	.....	1.8
1860	Peak	89.9	22.98	.....	16.8	2	8.4	.....
1862	Trough	93.7	.....	4.23	3.8	2	.....	1.9
1866	Peak	124.1	32.44	.....	30.4	4	7.6	.....
1868	Trough	126.6	.....	2.01	2.5	2	.....	1.2
1873	Peak	191.0	50.87	.....	64.4	5	12.9	.....
1879	Trough	212.2	.....	11.10	21.2	6	.....	3.5
1883	Peak	266.4	25.54	.....	54.2	4	13.6	.....
1886	Trough	254.6	.....	-4.43	-11.0	3	.....	-3.9
1890	Peak	303.1	19.05	.....	48.5	4	12.1	.....
1894	Trough	324.5	.....	7.06	21.4	4	.....	5.4
1900	Peak	424.9	30.94	.....	100.4	6	16.7	.....
1901	Trough	415.9	.....	-2.12	-9.0	1	.....	-9.0
1903	Peak	443.7	6.68	.....	27.8	2	13.9	.....
1904	Trough	449.9	.....	1.40	6.2	1	.....	6.2
1907	Peak	515.9	14.67	.....	66.0	3	22.0	.....
1908	Trough	491.6	.....	-4.71	-24.3	1	.....	-24.3
1913	Peak	568.2	15.58	.....	76.6	5	15.3	.....

[a] In tonnage conveyed, the weight of a shipment passing over several railroads is counted several times, once for each railroad. In tonnage originated (Table 1) it is counted only once.

CHART **3**

Ton-miles, All Commodities and All except Coal, Coke, and Patent Fuel
January 1920-April 1939

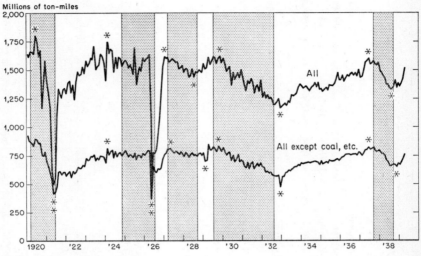

Shaded periods are reference contractions.

time to the reference contractions of 1883-86 and 1907-08. Tonnage also diminished during part of 1860-62, 1866-68, 1873-79 (only the last two years) and 1890-94. A decline in 1900-1901 continued beyond the end of the business phase. In the business contractions 1857-58 and 1903-1904, on the other hand, the amount of merchandise conveyed increased, but not as fast, in either case, as in the succeeding business expansion. If allowance is made for the rate as well as the direction of change, merchandise conformed positively to the reference chronology without exception (Table 3).[4]

Similarity of direction, however, is a closer kind of correspondence than rate of change. In this sense, before the war, even the changes in general merchandise traffic corresponded more closely to the changes in coal production than they did to the reference chronology. In 11 pairs of years for which we have traffic data, coal production fell while busi-

[4] For the reference chronology in monthly, quarterly and annual form, see Arthur F. Burns and Wesley C. Mitchell, *Measuring Business Cycles* (National Bureau of Economic Research, 1946), p. 78. The authors drew up an annual chronology in order to supplement their studies of monthly or quarterly data with data available only in annual form; if they had worked from annual data only they might have recognized fewer and somewhat differently dated cycles (pp. 81, 261-2).

8

TABLE 3

Tons of General Merchandise Conveyed
Change per Year between Reference Peaks and Troughs, 1857-1913

REFERENCE DATE	LEVEL OF BUSINESS	YEARS FROM PRECEDING DATE	TONS CARRIED	CHANGE FROM PRECEDING DATE Per year	To peak from trough	To trough from peak
				Total		
			(millions of tons)			
1857	Peak	....	25.0	....	....	....
1858	Trough	1	25.6	0.6	....	0.6
1860	Peak	2	29.5	3.9	2.0	....
1862	Trough	2	30.3	0.8	....	0.4
1866	Peak	4	38.6	8.3	2.1	....
1868	Trough	2	39.6	1.0	....	0.5
1873	Peak	5	60.9	21.3	4.3	....
1879	Trough	6	62.9	2.0	....	0.3
1883	Peak	4	76.9	14.0	3.5	....
1886	Trough	3	72.7	−4.2	....	−1.4
1890	Peak	4	87.3	14.6	3.6	....
1894	Trough	4	90.1	2.8	....	0.7
1900	Peak	6	118.5	28.4	4.7	....
1901	Trough	1	117.9	−0.6	....	−0.6
1903	Peak	2	100.0[a]	[a]	[a]	....
1904	Trough	1	100.3	0.3	....	0.3
1907	Peak	3	108.3	8.0	2.7	....
1908	Trough	1	103.2	−5.1	....	−5.1
1913	Peak	5	121.4	18.2	3.6	....

[a] 1903 figure not comparable with previous years; rate of change 1901-03 not comparable with 1903-04.

ness expanded, or vice versa. In 8 of these instances, merchandise followed coal rather than general business activity.[5]

Was railway participation inversely related to the state of trade?

Although railway traffic is positively related to the total flow of commodities, the relation is not necessarily constant. Both domestic produc-

[5] The eight instances are 1860-61, 1866-67, 1874-75, 1875-76, 1876-77, 1890-91, 1893-94, 1903-04. The other three are 1856-57, 1878-79, 1911-12. In 1897-98 business was expanding but coal production was 202.1 million tons in both years.

CHART 4

Coal, Coke, and Patent Fuel
Ratio of Tonnage Originated by Railways to Total Supply
1921-1938

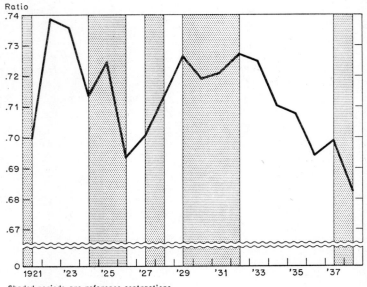

Shaded periods are reference contractions.

tion and imports can be disposed of in ways which do not involve rail movement. The percentage share of the railroads in total flow may fluctuate with business conditions. We have endeavored to find out whether it has done so in recent years. (The necessary data are not available for earlier times. Since 1920 the alternatives to rail shipment have been greatly expanded by the development of motor transport facilities.)

The ratio of railway tonnage of coal, coke, and patent fuel to the total supply of these commodities has ranged from 68 to 74 per cent since 1921 (Chart 4).[6] In 1921-24 and 1929-32 there was considerable fluctuation within the phase. No consistent contrast between expansions and contractions in direction of movement strikes the eye. Thus there was a net rise in 1921-24, a net fall in 1924-26. Although the ratio

[6] Supply = production of coal, coke (at coke plants and at gas works) and manufactured fuel, plus imports of coal, coke ("gas" and "other sorts"), and manufactured fuel. Data from Secretary of Mines: *Annual Report* and *Statistical Abstract*. Gas house coke in 1921 estimated by applying to the 1921 coal used the 1922-26 average ratio of coke produced to coal used.

declined in 1932-37, it did so less rapidly than in 1937-38. On the other hand the rate of rise in 1927-28 is slightly greater than in 1926-27. The ratio conformed inversely in the peak-to-peak cycle 1929-37, showing a slight net rise in the contraction and a marked fall in the expansion. All in all, we can hardly say that the railway share in the disposal of these important commodities was consistently related to business conditions.

For other commodities in the aggregate, we do not have enough data for similar comparisons. We have, however, been able to construct at least crude measures of the total flow of thirteen commodities from 1928 to 1938 (Table 4; for details, see the appended note on sources of data: supply of commodities. Production data for earlier years are so limited that we have not ventured to construct similar measures for them). These accounted for between 46 and 51 per cent of railway tonnage other than coal and coal products. From the 1928 traffic data and the supply estimates, we computed the tonnage of each commodity the railroads would have originated if their traffic had varied in proportion to supply since 1928 (Table 5). Finally we added these thirteen hypothetical figures and computed the ratio of the aggregate actual to the aggregate hypothetical tonnages originated. It declined steadily throughout the period (Chart 5). But in 1928-29 the fall was less rapid than in 1929-32 and in 1932-37 it was decidedly less steep than in either 1929-32 or 1937-38. The data suggest that the railroads tend to lose part of their share in the disposal of commodities other than coal, etc. to other outlets in business contraction and to regain it in expansion. Progressive improvement of highways and motor trucks, and growing familiarity of traders with the possibilities of this comparatively new means of transport, prevented the railway companies from regaining their share in 1928-29 or 1932-37. But general business expansion did slow up the process of diversion.[7]

Fluctuations of traffic varied in length and cmplitude

Judging from annual figures, some of the disturbances in rail traffic itself (i.e. those measured between high and low points in tonnage

[7] Not all of the loss in relative position should be attributed to highway developments. Reorganization of the iron and steel industry, for example, may have eliminated some interplant transport entirely. See Import Duties Advisory Committee, *Report on the Present Position and Future Development of the Iron and Steel Industry* (1937), pp. 42-3.

TABLE **4**
Supply of Thirteen Groups of Commodities, 1928-1938
(thousands of tons)

GROUP NUMBER	COMMODITY	1928	1929	1930	1931	1932	1933	1934	1935	1936	1937	1938
1	Creosote, tar, and pitch	2,352	2,537	2,338	1,990	1,950	2,075	2,287	2,350	2,565	2,764	2,680
2	Grain, flour, and milling offals	15,296	15,764	14,585	16,221	15,490	16,358	16,617	16,435	16,637	16,287	16,659
3	Gravel and sand	5,420	6,288	7,674	8,654	8,083	9,894	11,824	13,370	15,688	17,924	19,252
4	Iron ore	15,656	18,840	15,714	9,734	9,094	10,161	14,900	15,398	18,621	21,168	16,961
5	Iron and steel blooms, billets, and ingots	9,042	10,082	7,749	5,626	5,511	7,129	9,001	9,927	12,002	13,171	10,490
6	Iron and steel, other descriptions	11,365	12,346	9,960	7,762	6,706	7,876	10,059	10,889	12,963	14,333	11,319
7	Limestone and chalk	14,879	16,199	15,673	14,008	12,693	13,905	16,332	17,483	19,208	21,959	21,470
8	Oil cake	1,284	1,364	1,137	1,240	1,216	1,112	1,307	1,469	1,364	1,537	1,544
9	Pig iron	6,557	7,533	6,350	3,988	3,662	4,180	6,000	6,397	7,820	8,984	7,026
10	Road-making and road-repairing material	14,263	14,728	16,440	18,489	16,153	16,065	17,385	18,002	20,408	21,763	22,634
11	Timber	7,090	7,690	7,513	6,112	6,091	7,272	8,408	7,960	8,725	9,430	6,819
12	Potatoes	5,021	5,036	3,892	3,987	5,228	4,751	4,618	3,956	4,120	4,270	4,550
13	Vegetables, other than potatoes	24,151	23,022	22,667	18,991	20,316	18,793	18,544	18,734	20,215	16,880	16,856

CHART 5

Ratio of Annual Tonnage Originated by Railways to 1928 Tonnage
Adjusted for Changes in Supply
Thirteen Groups of Commodities, 1928-1938

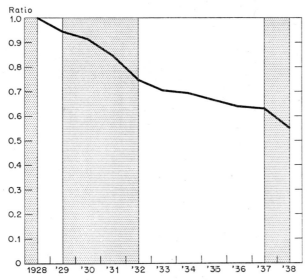

Shaded periods are reference contractions.

rather than between reference dates) have lasted much longer or
attained greater proportions than others (Table 6). Some phases en-
dured about a year; one expansion continued for seven years and several
contractions for three. From 1928 to 1929, tonnage increased 8 per
cent, from 1868 to 1873, 51 per cent. Declines ranged from 1 per cent
in 1861-62 to 24 per cent in 1929-32. If we add the slight 1908-11 rise
(which some observers might prefer to regard as merely a part of a
1908-13 expansion of 16 per cent) at one end of the scale, and phases
which owe part of their amplitude to the great strikes at the other, the
range becomes even greater.[8]

[8] The percentages for expansions are not comparable with those for contractions, of
course, since, e.g., a change from 100 to 200 million tons is a 100 per cent rise, but
a change from 200 to 100 million is a 50 per cent fall.

   Monthly figures would yield larger amplitudes between approximately the same
dates. On the other hand, if such data could be substituted, the six-year expansion
1901-1907 might break up into three smaller phases.

TABLE 5

Hypothetical and Actual Tons Originated, Thirteen Commodity Groups, 1928-1938
(thousands of tons)

LINE NUMBER	1928	1929	1930	1931	1932	1933	1934	1935	1936	1937	1938
1	1,983	2,139	1,971	1,678	1,644	1,750	1,928	1,981	2,162	2,331	2,260
2	6,223	6,413	5,934	6,599	6,302	6,655	6,761	6,687	6,769	6,626	6,777
3	3,336	3,870	4,723	5,327	4,975	6,090	7,277	8,229	9,656	11,032	11,983
4	10,587	12,739	10,626	6,583	6,150	6,871	10,076	10,412	12,592	14,314	11,469
5	3,322	3,704	2,847	2,067	2,025	2,619	3,307	3,647	4,409	4,839	3,854
6	8,883	9,650	7,785	6,067	5,242	6,156	7,862	8,511	10,132	11,203	8,847
7	5,026	5,472	5,294	4,732	4,288	4,697	5,517	5,906	6,489	7,417	7,253
8	1,176	1,250	1,042	1,136	1,114	1,019	1,197	1,346	1,250	1,408	1,414
9	3,624	4,163	3,509	2,204	2,024	2,310	3,316	3,536	4,322	4,965	3,883
10	8,892	9,182	10,249	11,527	10,070	10,015	10,838	11,223	12,723	13,567	14,111
11	5,789	6,278	6,134	4,990	4,973	5,938	6,865	6,499	7,123	7,699	5,568
12	1,638	1,643	1,270	1,301	1,765	1,550	1,506	1,290	1,344	1,393	1,484
13	1,371	1,307	1,287	1,078	1,153	1,067	1,053	1,063	1,148	958	957
14	61,850	67,810	62,671	55,289	51,665	56,737	67,503	70,330	80,119	87,752	79,860
15	61,850	64,161	57,251	46,787	38,711	39,892	46,822	46,773	51,070	55,308	44,032
16	1.0000	.9462	.9135	.8462	.7493	.7031	.6936	.6651	.6374	.6303	.5514
17	121,283	124,815	113,336	96,628	84,186	87,203	97,614	97,675	104,867	110,525	92,984
18	.51	.51	.51	.48	.46	.46	.48	.48	.49	.50	.47

14

Line
(1-13) Each computed as follows: supply figures on corresponding line, Table 4, divided by 1928 figure, same line, that table. Actual railway tonnage, 1928, multiplied by resulting ratio for each later year.
(14) Total, lines 1-13.
(15) Actual revenue tons originated, 13 commodity groups.
(16) Ratio of actual to hypothetical, line 15 ÷ line 14.
(17) Actual revenue tons originated, all commodities except coal, coke, and patent fuel.
(18) Ratio of actual, 13 commodity groups, to actual, all commodities except coal, etc. line 15 ÷ line 17.

TABLE 6

Expansions and Contractions in Tons of Merchandise and Minerals Conveyed, 1861-1913; Originated, 1920-1938[a] Duration and Percentage Change (Annual Data)

DURATION (YEARS)				PERCENTAGE CHANGE			
EXPANSIONS		CONTRACTIONS		EXPANSIONS		CONTRACTIONS	
					Per		Per
Dates	Duration	Dates	Duration	Dates	Cent	Dates	Cent
1893-1900	7	1883-86	3	1921-23	58	1923-26	−37
1901-07	6	1923-26	3	1862-67[a]	55	1920-21	−31
1862-67	5	1929-32	3	1868-73	51	1929-32	−24
1868-73[b]	5	1891-93	2	1926-27	49	1867-68[b]	−13
1878-83	5	1861-62	1	1893-1900	45	1937-38	−11
1886-91	5	1867-68[b]	1	1878-83	29	1891-93	−5
1932-37	5	1873-74	1	1901-07	24	1907-08	−5
1874-77	3	1877-78	1	1886-91	22	1927-28	−5
1908-11	3	1900-01	1	1932-37	19	1883-86	−4
1921-23	2	1907-08	1	1874-77	12	1877-78	−2
1912-13[b]	1	1911-12	1	1912-13[b]	9	1900-01	−2
1926-27	1	1920-21	1	1928-29	8	1861-62	−1
1928-29	1	1927-28	1	1908-11	7	1873-74	−1
		1937-38	1			1911-12	−1

[a] Livestock excluded, 1861-1921; included, 1921-38.
[b] 1868 assumed to be a trough and 1913 a peak because of level of coal production.

Greater growth from cycle to cycle in earlier times

Before World War I traffic contractions were merely rather mild interruptions in a history of persistent growth. Traffic lost in such a phase was regained or more than regained in a year or so, and substantially more than regained by the end of the following expansion (Chart 1).

After the war, on the other hand, each cycle attained about the same high level as, or one somewhat lower than, its predecessor (Chart 3). The cessation of growth in rail traffic from cycle to cycle is explained, at least in part, by the increasing comparative attractiveness of a new means of transport, the motor truck. At the beginning of registration statistics in 1922, there were only 133,000 commercial goods vehicles in Britain; the number (seasonally adjusted, as usual in this paper) rose steadily to 488,000 at the outbreak of World War II (cf. Chart 6).

Proportion of durables rose and fell with business

Production of durable goods and of commodities used in making them generally fluctuates more over the course of a cycle than that of other goods. If it did so in Britain from 1920 to 1938, we should expect similar changes in the composition of freight traffic. We cannot make a complete count of durables tonnage, since the statistics classify only about two-thirds of the freight other than coal. But the ratio of such

CHART 6

Motor Cars, Motor Cycles, and Commercial Goods Vehicles with Licenses Current, 1922-1952
(At end of February, May, August, and November)

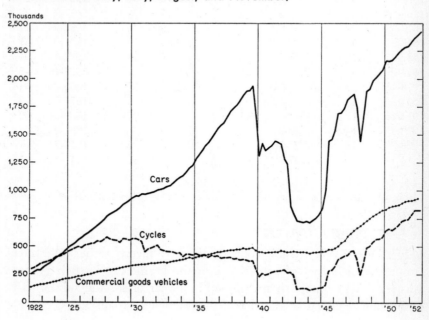

16

durables as there are figures for did tend to rise in expansion and fall in contraction (Chart 7, lower group of curves). Between 1923 and 1938, however, the relation is obscured. The ratio increased in 1924-26, diminished in 1926-27, apparently increased a little in 1927-28, declined in 1928-29. But the rise in 1924-26 was less rapid than in 1921-24, the fall in 1928-29 less precipitous than in 1929-32. It may be that the range of articles included in durables broadened from 1927 to 1928; we are therefore uncertain how to interpret the seeming rise in that contraction.[9]

In the foregoing comparisons, coal, etc. is included in total traffic. After 1927, changes in coal tonnage originated reflected primarily cyclical variations in the demand for that commodity. In the phases between 1921 and 1927, the dominant cause of the decline in coal traffic was the cutting off of supplies by the strike. To be sure, the shortage of fuel severely curtailed the production and shipment of other commodities, including those important durables, iron and steel. But the disturbance in iron and steel was not as severe as in coal (Table 7). The strikes tended to raise the ratio of durables to all freight, including coal. The ratio of durables to all traffic except coal was more consistently related to business fluctuations. It rose and fell in accordance with business in all phases except, perhaps, 1927-28 (Chart 7, upper curve). The first trough also coincided with that in business instead of coming a year later as in the case of the ratio to all traffic including coal.

[9] The categories are as follows (identity of language does not guarantee identical content as between the two groups of years) :

1920-27	1928-38
Bricks	Bricks, blocks, and tiles
Cement, plaster, and whiting	Cement and lime
Gravel and sand	Gravel and sand
Iron and steel	Iron and steel blooms, billets, and ingots, etc.
	Iron and steel, other descriptions
	Iron and steel scrap
Ironstone and iron ore	Iron ore
Limestone (other than road-making or agricultural)	Limestone and chalk
Pig iron	Pig iron
Stone and other material for road-making	Road-making and road-repairing material
Timber	Timber

The Ministry of Transport failed to obtain data on cement, plaster, and whiting for 1926; hence comparable figures for 1924-26 and its adjoining phases must exclude these articles.

17

TABLE 7

Production Measures and Ton-Miles

Per Cent Change in Each between its Peaks and Troughs or Quasi-Troughs, 1920-1938

	PEAK 1920	QUASI-TROUGH Before 1921 strike	QUASI-TROUGH After 1921 strike	PEAK 1923 (except as noted)	QUASI-TROUGH 1925	PEAK 1927	TROUGH 1928	PEAK 1929	TROUGH 1932 (except as noted)	PEAK 1937	TROUGH 1938
Production of coal											
Date	June	Feb.	Aug.	June	Aug.	July	April	June	June, 1933	April	Dec.
Amount, millions of tons per week[a]	4.77	4.03	4.23	5.51	4.53	5.10	4.59	5.12	3.94	4.75	4.42
Production of steel ingots and castings											
Date	Sept.	Feb.	Sept.	June	Aug.	April	April	Aug.	Sept, 1931	Dec.	July
Amount, thousands of tons[b]	745	436	443	724	601	835	679	852	420	1161	754
Production, industrial											
Date	[c]	[c]	3Q	3Q 1924	3Q	3Q	3Q	3Q	2Q 1931	2Q	3Q
Index, 1924 = 100[d]	.....	.....	90.3	102.0	93.9	110.3	99.4	112.7	80.6	126.5	103.4
Ton-miles, coal, etc.											
Date	June	Feb.	Aug.	June	Aug.	Jan.	July	Mar.	April, 1933	May	May
Amount, millions	853	652	676	866	766	830	713	794	600	775	675

Ton-miles, other											
Date	[c]	[c]	Sept.	Feb., 1924	Aug.	May	Feb., 1929	Oct.	Dec.	June	Nov.
Amount, millions	[c]	[c]	602	750	750	801	726	808	540	809	668
Ton-miles, total											
Date	June	Feb.	Aug.	Feb., 1924	Aug.	Jan.	July	Nov.	Dec.	June	Aug.
Amount, millions	1729	1294	1245	1598	1516	1584	1476	1595	1198	1575	1339
% change in amount or index, from preceding date											
Production of coal	......	−16	......	30	−18	13	−10	12	−23	21	−7
Production of steel ingots and castings	......	−41	......	63	−17	39	−19	25	−51	176	−35
Production, industrial	......	......	......	13	−8	17	−10	13	−28	57	−18
Ton-miles, coal, etc.	......	−24	......	28	−12	8	−14	11	−24	29	−13
Ton-miles, other	......	......	......	25	0	7	−9	11	−33	50	−17
Ton-miles, total	......	−25	......	28	−5	4	−7	8	−25	31	−15

[a] Computed from data in *Board of Trade Journal*, various issues, and Secretary of Mines, *Annual Report*, 1926, p. 82. Each of the underlying monthly figures is an average of four or five weekly figures. Weeks ending on first, second or third day of a month are assigned to the previous month.

[b] From various issues of *The Iron and Coal Trade Review*.

[c] Peak not determinable; cf. Chart 3.

[d] From London and Cambridge Economic Service, *Monthly Bulletin*, various issues. Prepared by J. F. W. Rowe. Data are quarterly.

Amounts are averages for month indicated, preceding and following month, e.g. 853 million ton-miles is average coal ton-miles in May, June, and July, 1920.

The two kinds of ton-miles do not add up exactly to the total, as the seasonal adjustment was carried out separately for each of the three sets of figures.

19

Fluctuations in traffic normally were moderate

Cyclical fluctuations in railway freight traffic are normally much less severe than those in the production of durable goods. We can illustrate the difference by comparing ton-miles with the production of steel ingots and castings. But first we must note that the business cycles between 1920 and 1926 were peculiar in that the contractions were marked off from the expansion by two great strikes. The first of these, in 1921, centered in the coal industry but affected other industries by cutting off their supply of fuel. The second was more general. We shall begin our discussion with the cycles between 1927 and 1938, which are free of this complication.

In that later period, fluctuations in coal production were milder, percentagewise, than those in steel production (Table 7, last 6 columns). Coal is used not only to produce durable goods, but to produce

CHART 7

Percentage Ratio of Tons of Selected Durable Commodities to Total Tons Originated, 1920-1938

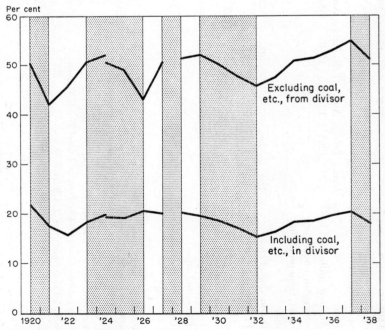

Shaded periods are contractions in total tons originated.
9 durables, 1921-24; 8, 1924-27; 11, 1928-38.

20

nondurable goods, to generate electricity, which in turn serves a great variety of purposes, and to heat buildings; many of these uses are quite stable. Fluctuations in coal ton-miles, although not identical with those in coal production, were likewise milder than those in ingot production. Ton-miles other than coal include the movement of nondurables as well as durables; fluctuations in "other" ton-miles were likewise mild compared with those in steel production.

As to the strike cycles, consideration of Charts 2 and 3 and of a similar chart for ingots suggests that the effects of the first strike were felt from April through June 1921 (with some lag in the case of steel production and "other" ton-miles) and that the effects of the second were felt from May through December 1926. The strikes depressed all six aspects of economic activity, but affected some much more than others (Table 8). The mining of coal practically ceased. Its movement was maintained better than its production — imports and stocks must have moved by rail — but coal ton-miles diminished much more than industrial production or other ton-miles. Ingot production did not fall quite as far as coal production, but the loss of fuel nevertheless closed the steel industry down almost completely.

If we were to compare the percentage decline in, say, the movement of coal from its 1920 peak to its absolute trough in 1921 with the percentage decline in some other economic activity, the outcome of our comparison would be influenced by the peculiar effects of the strike on amplitudes of fluctuation. But the decline from 1920 to the *verge* of the strike period, and the rise from the first few months after the strike period to the peak in 1923 (or 1924), is free from this distortion. We may take the last three months before the strike period as a quasi-trough for comparison with 1920, and the first three months after it as a quasi-trough for comparison with 1923 (or 1924).

A similar procedure would not work in the vicinity of the 1926 strike. The economic activities considered did not decline steadily from their 1923 or 1924 peaks to the verge of the strike. On the contrary, all of them showed an upturn after August 1925. Their level in the three months just before the strike differed little from their level at their respective 1923 or 1924 peaks, and their level immediately after the strike differed even less from their level at their 1927 peaks. We therefore take the third quarter of 1925 as a quasi-trough. We measure the percentage drop in each activity from its 1923 (or 1924) peak to this

21

TABLE 8
Production Measures and Ton-Miles before, during, and after
Periods of Strike Disturbance, 1921 and 1926

	Three preceding months (1)	Three lowest months (2)	Three following months (3)	PER CENT (2) of (1) (4)	PER CENT (2) of (3) (5)
		AVERAGES FOR			
1921					
Months included	Jan., Feb., March	April, May, June[a]	July, Aug., Sept.[b]		
Production of coal	4.03	0.06	4.23	1	1
Production of steel ingots and castings	436	27	443	6	6
Production, industrial	87.8	54.4	90.3	62	60
Ton-miles, coal	652	96	676	15	14
Ton-miles, other	595	442	602	74	73
Ton-miles, total	1,294	559	1,245	43	45
1926					
Months included	Feb., March, April	May, June, July	Jan., Feb., March, 1927		
Production of coal	5.01	0.06	4.90	1	1
Production of steel ingots and castings	680	36	802	5	4
Ton-miles, coal	825	123	826	15	15
Ton-miles, other	789	542	782	69	69
Ton-miles, total	1,614	665	1,608	41	41

[a] For "other" ton-miles, May, June, July.

[b] For steel ingots and "other" ton-miles, August, September, October.

For sources and units of measurement, see Table 7. The quarterly data of the industrial production index do not fit the time pattern of the strike in 1926; the index is therefore not shown for 1926.

quasi-trough, and its net percentage rise from the quasi-trough to its 1927 peak.

The data for peaks and quasi-troughs, 1920-27 (Table 7, first six columns) yield conclusions like those derived from the data for peaks and troughs, 1927-38. Again the downswings and upswings in total traffic are less severe, percentagewise, than those in steel production; they are closer, in amplitude, to those in general industrial production.

2. The Movement of Persons

Number of journeys was related to the state of business

In almost every year from 1850 to 1912, the British and their visitors took more railway journeys than they did the year before (Tables 9, 17). There were only three slight declines — 0.4 per cent from 1878 to 1879, 1.0 per cent from 1908 to 1909, and 2.4 per cent from 1911 to 1912. The first of these could be regarded as a brief eventual response to the business contraction of 1873-79, the second as a belated reaction to the contraction of 1907-08. The third cannot plausibly be paired with any phase in the reference chronology: it was probably a consequence of the coal strike in 1912. With two exceptions, then, we cannot find any specific phases corresponding with the prewar business phases[1] (monthly figures, if we had any, might show a closer relation). Growth, however, was retarded in all the business contractions except 1890-94 (Table 10). Even in that instance the average annual increase, while slightly larger than in the preceding, was much smaller than in the following expansion.[2]

After the war, the response of potential travelers to business conditions was much more conspicuous. For every reference phase, annual figures, which include the numerous routine journeys of season ticket holders, reveal a rise in the number of journeys for every business expan-

[1] There is no complete figure for 1868. But even the incomplete total shows a rise from 1867. Conceivably travel may have diminished from 1868 to 1869; 1866-68 is a reference contraction.

[2] Production of pig iron and steel ingots was smaller in 1893 than in 1894. The trough year in coal production, cotton imports, consumption of rails, tonnage of vessels entered, and tonnage cleared was 1893 rather than 1894. If 1893 is taken as a reference trough, the growth of passenger traffic per year is as follows (millions of journeys):

1886-90	23 0
1890-93	18.5
1893-1900	38.4

This single exception to the general pattern of retarded growth disappears.

TABLE 9

Number of Rail Journeys, 1845-1902
(millions)

1845	33.8[a]	1873	455.3
1846	43.8[a]	1874	477.8
1847	51.4[a]	1875	507.0
1848	58.0[a]	1876	534.5
1849	60.4[a]	1877	549.5
		1878	565.0
1849	63.8	1879	562.7
1850	72.9	1880	603.9
1851	85.4	1881	626.0
1852	89.1	1882	654.8
1853	102.3	1883	683.7
1854	111.2	1884	695.0
1855	118.6	1885	697.2
1856	129.3	1886	725.6
1857	139.0	1887	733.7
1858	139.1	1888	742.5
1859	149.8	1889	775.2
1860	163.4	1890	817.7
1861	173.7	1891	845.5
1862	180.4	1892	864.4
1863	204.6	1893	873.2
1864	229.3	1894	911.4
1865	251.9	1895	929.8
1866	274.3	1896	980.3
1867	287.7	1897	1030.4
1868	304.1[b]	1898	1062.9
1869	306.7	1899	1106.7
1870	336.5	1900	1142.3
1871	375.2	1901	1172.4
1872	422.9	1902	1188.2

[a] Years ended June 30.

[b] Incomplete: some companies failed to report.

Does not include journeys by holders of season and periodical tickets. No information on such tickets, 1845-50. Number of holders reported beginning 1851, but each holder counted as one regardless of length of time for which ticket was valid, 1851-1901, number of journeys cannot be estimated. For number, 1902-13, including and excluding holders of season tickets, see Table 17.

TABLE **10**

Rail Journeys: Change per Year between Reference Years, 1854-1913

REFERENCE DATE	LEVEL OF BUSINESS	YEARS FROM PRECEDING DATE	NUMBER OF JOURNEYS[a]	CHANGE FROM PRECEDING DATE		
					Per year	
				Total	*To peak from trough*	*To trough from peak*
				(m i l l i o n s)		
1854[b]	Peak	....	111.2	......	......	......
1855	Trough	1	118.6	7.4	......	7.4
1857	Peak	2	139.0	20.4	10.2	......
1858	Trough	1	139.1	0.1	......	0.1
1860	Peak	2	163.4	24.3	12.2	......
1862	Trough	2	180.4	17.0	......	8.5
1866	Peak	4	274.3	93.9	23.5	......
1868	Trough	2	c	c	......	c
1873	Peak	5	455.3	c	c	......
1879	Trough	6	562.7	107.4	......	17.9
1883	Peak	4	683.7	121.0	30.2	......
1886	Trough	3	725.6	41.9	......	14.0
1890	Peak	4	817.7	92.1	23.0	......
1894	Trough	4	911.4	93.7	......	23.4
1900	Peak	6	1142.3	230.9	38.5	......
1901	Trough	1	1172.4	30.1	......	30.1
1903	Peak	2	1195.3	22.9	11.4	......
1904	Trough	1	1198.8	3.5	......	3.5
1907	Peak	3	1259.5	60.7	20.2	......
1908	Trough	1	1278.1	18.6	......	18.6
1903	Peak	....	1566.1	......	......	......
1904	Trough	1	1585.1	19.0	......	19.0
1907	Peak	3	1688.9	103.8	34.6	......
1908	Trough	1	1711.2	22.3	......	22.3
1913	Peak	5	1897.5	186.3	37.3	......

[a] Journeys of season ticket holders included only in lower (1903-13) segment. Not shown for reference peak 1845 or trough 1848, since reference dates pertain to calendar, data to fiscal years.

[b] Earliest reference date for which calendar year data on journeys are available; no reference dates available on fiscal year basis.

[c] No data for 1868; no computation possible for 1866-68 or 1868-73.

sion, a fall for every contraction (Chart 8, top line).[3] The expansion corresponding to the 1921-23 reference phase was, to be sure, short and small. War conditions, severely discouraging ordinary civilian travel, prolonged and in 1940 greatly deepened the contraction after 1937. (The most rapid growth of military and other war-connected travel came after 1940.)

Monthly data, which do not include the trips of season ticket holders, fail to disclose any specific contraction in the vicinity of 1927-28 (Chart 9). But the curve is flatter in that reference phase than in the expansion before or after. And all the other reference phases from 1920 to 1938 can be matched by rises and falls in journeys. (Because we have no monthly figures before July 1920 or after April 1939, we cannot fix the beginning of the first or the end of the last contraction.)

In May 1937, many people must have gone up to London to see the coronation ceremonies; the number of travellers was enormous. Had there been no change of kings, May would not have towered so far above its neighboring months; but it or some one of them would have been a peak, and there would still have been a rise from 1932 to 1937 and a decline thereafter.

In the subways of London, the traffic of May 1937 was even more memorable. Busmen in the central area of the city went on strike. All busses in that area were completely withdrawn from service from May 1 to May 27 inclusive.[4] The combination of the ceremonies and the absence of alternative facilities created an enormous jam below ground (Chart 9). If these dramatic but transient events had not occurred, it looks as though May would have been lower than subsequent months, and we accordingly place the peak in December. Another royal ritual — a silver jubilee — crowded the underground lines in May 1935.[5] In March 1924 a strike of tramwaymen and busmen diverted a heavy traffic from the surface lines.[6]

[3] The number of season tickets is reported in terms of equivalent annual tickets, e.g. a ticket usable for three months is counted as one-fourth of a ticket. It is assumed that each annual equivalent ticket is used for a return trip on each of 300 days, i.e. for 600 journeys.

Rides on London underground railways are not included.

All figures are for passengers originating; a passenger travelling over several railroads is counted only once.

[4] London Passenger Transport Board, *Annual Report,* year ended June 30, 1937, p. 9.

[5] London Passenger Transport Board, *Annual Report,* year ended June 30, 1935, p. 25; *Railway Gazette,* May 17, 1935, p. 953.

[6] *Railway Gazette,* March 28, 1924, p. 488.

CHART 8

Rail Journeys: On Season Tickets, Other, and Total, 1919-1951

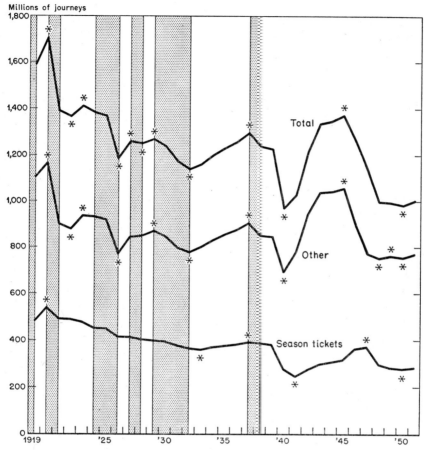

Shaded periods are reference contractions.

For the purpose of fixing peaks and troughs, we ignore the salient fluctuations that reflect these accidental circumstances. We are able to discern broader waves in the number of underground rides, which correspond on the whole to the reference chronology. Again there is no contraction in the vicinity of 1927-28; but the growth in that business contraction was less rapid than in 1926-27 or 1928-29 (Table 11). All the other reference phases can be matched with specific increases and declines. For lack of monthly figures, the starting date of the first contraction in rides and the ending date of the last cannot be fixed.

27

TABLE **11**

London Underground Rides
Change per Month between Reference Months, 1926-1929

| | | | | CHANGE FROM PRECEDING DATE | | |
| | | | | | Per month | |
REFERENCE DATE	LEVEL OF BUSINESS	MONTHS FROM PRECEDING DATE	NUMBER OF RIDES[a]	Total	To peak from trough	To trough from peak
				(m i l l i o n s)		
July 1926	Trough	....	24.9	....	......	......
March 1927	Peak	8	27.7	2.8	0.35	......
Sept. 1928	Trough	18	29.7	2.0	......	0.11
July 1929	Peak	10	31.7	2.0	0.20	......

[a] Three-month average.

Riding on trams (street cars) and trolley-busses also fluctuated with business (Chart 10).[7] From 1920 to 1929 traffic increased and decreased in rough correspondence with the reference phases. Except for a slight rise, 1935-36, however, there was no traffic expansion corresponding to the 1932-37 business expansion. But the flatness of the curve during that reference phase makes a sharp contrast with its abrupt fall in 1929-32. During the whole period from 1920, an eventually large part of the service initially provided by trams was taken over by motor busses. We would prefer to study the total of tram, etc. and bus passengers, but unfortunately no figures including the latter are available before 1932. The combined total did rise from 1932 to 1937 (Table 12, column 10).

Growth of motor competition

For the railways, the growing appeal of travel by private motor car was probably of greater moment than the growth of travel by bus. From 1922 to the outbreak of war seventeen years later, car ownership in-

[7] From Table 12, column 8. The average ending date of the year, weighted by the amount of traffic reported in connection with each ending date, would be slightly before March 31 prior to 1932 and somewhat later than March 31 in later years. Our usual practice is to chart a figure in the middle of the period to which it pertains. Accordingly we have plotted the data at September 30 of the calendar year opposite which they are shown in the table, through 1931, and a little later beginning 1932.

CHART 9

Rail Journeys, July 1920-April 1939

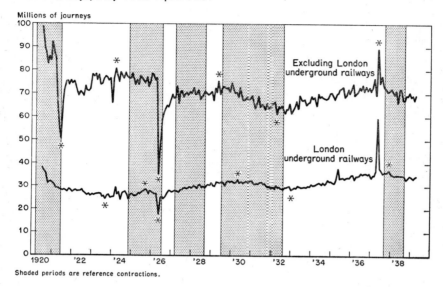

Millions of journeys

Shaded periods are reference contractions.

CHART 10

Rides on Trams and Trolley Vehicles, 1920-1937

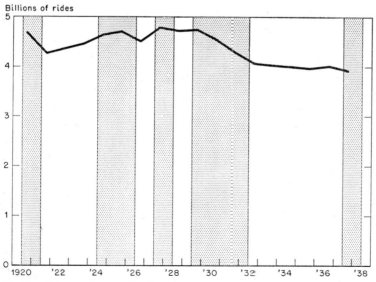

Billions of rides

Shaded periods are reference contractions

TABLE **12**

Rides on Trams and Trolley Vehicles, 1920-1937
and on Trams, Trolley Vehicles and Busses, 1932-1937
(millions)

| CALENDAR YEAR | PRIVATE COMPANIES[a] | | PUBLIC AUTHORITIES[b] | | LONDON PASSENGER TRANSPORT BOARD[c] | | TOTAL Tram and Trolley Vehicles | Motor Busses, Calendar Year | TOTAL |
| | Trams | Trolley vehicles | Trams | Trolley vehicles | Trams | Trolley busses | (Cols. 2-7) | | Cols. (8) + (9) |
(1)	(2)	(3)	(4)	(5)	(6)	(7)	(8)	(9)	(10)
1920	821	d	3,848	11			4,680		
1921	699	d	3,558	10			4,267		
1922	655	1	3,694	11			4,361		
1923	660	1	3,784	18			4,462		
1924	645	1	3,976	23			4,645		
1925	604	1	4,065	33			4,703		
1926	545	1	3,916	50			4,512		
1927	565	1	4,140	79			4,785		
1928	545	7	4,078	92			4,722		
1929	520	19	4,094	108			4,741		
1930	503	24	3,892	129			4,548		
1931	447	39	3,660	145			4,291		
1932	398	60	3,447	161			4,066	5,345	9,411
1933[e]	197	41	2,578	186	1,002	27	4,031	5,424	9,455
1934	172	54	2,479	255	1,013	28	4,001	5,722	9,723
1935	165	56	2,378	320	983	70	3,972	6,031	10,003
1936	156	61	2,319	368	904	203	4,011	6,427	10,438
1937	111	64	2,247	433	701	368	3,924	6,664	10,588

NOTES TO TABLE 12

ª Calendar Year.
ᵇ Year ending March 31 following year in Col. 1.
ᶜ Year ending June 30 following year in Col. 1.
ᵈ Less than 500,000.
ᵉ The drop in the figures in cols. (2) to (4) reflects the transfer of many undertakings to the LPTB; their traffic even in the fraction of a year before the date of transfer is not included.
Cols. (2) to (5) from Ministry of Transport, *Tramways and Light Railways, Return of Capital, etc.* (annual), various issues. (6) and (7) from London Passenger Transport Board, *Annual Report and Accounts*, 1939. (9) from Traffic Commissioners' *Annual Report*, 1937-38.

creased continually — even in the contraction years 1930-32, although less rapidly then than before or after (Chart 6). A humbler form of private transport, motorcycling, gained in popularity up to the middle of 1928; but even before that date cars were increasingly preferred to cycles, and after it the number of the latter gradually declined. The growth of motoring can be discerned also in the swiftly rising consumption of motor fuel (Table 13). The figures, however, include consumption by all kinds of motor vehicles, not only cars. Meanwhile, rail travel, which grew so steadily before World War I, diminished or stagnated from one business cycle to the next. Business expansion in 1921-24 and 1926-27 did not restore to the railway companies all the passengers they had lost in contraction; there was little if any net gain from 1927 to 1929, or from 1929 to 1937.

Travel less volatile than tonnage

Although riding on railways and tramways was affected by business conditions, the disturbances were not as great as those in freight traffic. Between 1920 and 1938 the percentage fluctuations in the number of rail journeys (including those of season ticket holders but not rides on the London underground railways) were smaller than the most nearly corresponding specific changes in tonnage originated (Table 14. The one exception, resulting from the continued decline in rail journeys to 1940, may be ascribed to war conditions.) Percentage changes in the number of tram rides were likewise smaller than those in tonnage.

We are obliged to base the foregoing comparisons on annual figures, since regular monthly counts of railway journeys including those of season ticket holders have never been made, and there are no monthly figures on tram and trolley rides. We do have monthly data pertaining

TABLE **13**

Domestic Supply of Automotive Fuel (Motor Spirit), 1921-1951
(millions of gallons)

Year	Value	Year	Value
1921	238.7	1935	1,331.7
1922	284.6	1936	1,402.5
1923	287.6	1937	1,476.8
1924	379.2	1938	1,584.0
1925	358.5	1939	1,515.0
		1940	1,241.6
1925	485.9	1941	1,546.1
1926	677.0	1942	1,418.4
1927	702.9		
1928	823.6	1942	1,097.5
1929	870.0	1943	1,191.9
1930	1,057.3	1944	1,666.1
		1945	1,680.2
1930	1,095.8	1946	1,369.5
1931	1,047.0	1947	1,288.0
1932	1,092.3	1948	1,359.6
1933	1,199.5	1949	1,573.3
1934	1,241.5	1950	1,696.4
		1951	1,906.9

Computed from the following data, so far as available: (1) imports, (2) production of British refineries, (3) production in Britain from coal and shale, (4) imports re-exported, (5) domestic production exported.

1921-25 segment of table: (1)−(4).

1925-30 segment: (1)+(2)−(4)−(5).

1930-51 segments: (1)+(2)+(3)−(4)−(5). Aviation spirit excluded from (1) and (4) in 1942-51 segment, included previously.

(1), (4), and (5) from Customs and Excise Department, *Annual Statement of the Trade of the United Kingdom.* . . . In earlier years, (2) from Board of Trade Journal, e.g. June 6, 1935, p. 907; (3) from Mines Department, *Annual Report.* In later years, both from Central Statistical Office, *Annual Abstract of Statistics.*

to railway trips of passengers other than season ticket holders, and to rides on the underground. But they are not useful before 1929 or after 1937.[8] We therefore confine our comparisons to two phases (Table 15).

[8] Since we do not know when the peaks in travel corresponding to the 1920 peaks in ton-miles occurred, we cannot compute the decline from these peaks to the following troughs. Interpretation of comparative changes in 1921-26 would be complicated by the strikes. Furthermore, we would have to compare an expansion in ton-miles that began in 1921 and ended in February 1924 with an expansion in underground rides that did not begin until September 1923 and did not end until September 1925 — a comparison of doubtful meaning. There was no peak in either kind of travel until 1927 and no trough around 1928, so we have nothing to compare with the 1926-27 expansion, 1927-28 contraction, or 1928-29 expansion of freight traffic. We do not know when the contraction of travel that began in 1937 ended.

TABLE 14

Revenue Tons Originated, Railway Journeys, and Tram Rides
Per Cent Change between Specific Peak and Trough Years, 1920-1938

LEVEL OF TRAFFIC	TONS ORIGINATED[a]			RAIL JOURNEYS[b]			TRAM RIDES[c]		
	Date of level	Number (millions)	% change from preceding date	Date of level	Number (millions)	% change from preceding date	Date of level	Number (millions)	% change from preceding date
Peak	1920	318.6	.....	1920	1,704	.....	1920	4,680	.....
Trough	1921	219.9	−31	1922	1,366	−20	1921	4,267	−9
Peak	1923	347.9	58	1923	1,410	3	1925	4,703	10
Trough	1926	218.0	−37	1926	1,184	−16	1926	4,512	−4
Peak	1927	324.4	49	1927	1,257	6	1927	4,785	6
Trough	1928	308.6	−5	1928	1,250	1	1928	4,722	1
Peak	1929	331.9	8	1929	1,268	1	1929	4,741	[d]
Trough	1932	251.4	−24	1932	1,141	−10	1935	3,972	−16
Peak	1937	298.7	19	1937	1,295	13	1936	4,011	1[e]
Trough	1938	265.8	−11	1940	967	−25	f	f	f

[a] Including livestock.

[b] Including journeys of season ticket-holders but excluding London underground railways.

[c] Including rides on trolley vehicles. See Table 12.

[d] Increase, less than 0.5 per cent.

[e] Tram rides plus bus rides increased 13 per cent from 1932 to 1937.

[f] Not available.

33

In both, the changes in rail journeys and in underground rides were milder than those in ton-miles. Travelers are likely to take longer journeys in prosperous times. Passenger-miles may therefore vary more than the number of passengers. But American statistics indicate that variations in passenger-miles are also milder than those in ton-miles.

Since travel passed through few up-and-down fluctuations before

TABLE 15

Ton-Miles, Railway Journeys, and London Underground Rides
Per Cent Change between Specific Peak and Trough Months, 1921-1938

	TON-MILES[a] % Change from preceding date	RAIL JOURNEYS[b]		% Change from preceding date	UNDERGROUND RIDES		% Change from preceding date
LEVEL OF TRAFFIC		Date level reached	Number (millions)		Date level reached	Number (millions)	
Peak	......	May 1929	71.6	......	May 1930	32.0	....
Trough	—25	April 1932	64.0	—11	Jan. 1933	29.0	—9
Peak	31	May 1937	77.8	22	Dec. 1937	36.1	24

[a] For dates and absolute amounts see Table 7.
[b] Excluding those of season ticket holders and excluding London underground railways.

1913, we can't make phase-by-phase comparisons of amplitude in that earlier age. But in a sense we can say that then, too, passenger was more stable than freight traffic. Tonnage tended to increase more than the number of passengers in expansions, less in contractions (Table 16). In all 7 rising phases of business, both freight traffic and travel increased; but in 6 of them, the ratio of tons to passengers also rose, i.e. tonnage increased by a greater percentage than passengers. In 3 of 8 contractions, tonnage fell, but passengers became more numerous; the ratio, of course, fell. In 3 others, both kinds of traffic increased, but the ratio again fell — the rise in journeys was more vigorous than that in freight carried.

A similar conclusion emerges when we ask what happened to travel during the phases in freight traffic rather than during the reference phases. In all of the 7 freight expansions for which we know the number of passengers, the latter increased, but usually not in proportion to tonnage, for in 5 of them the ratio rose. In all the contractions of tonnage, journeys increased, and the ratio, of course, fell.

TABLE 16

Tons Conveyed, Number of Journeys, and Ratio of Tons to Journeys
Direction of Net Change between Reference Peak and Trough Years,
1857-1908
and between Peak and Trough Years in Tons Conveyed, 1861-1912

EXPANSIONS				CONTRACTIONS			
Dates	*Tons*	*Journeys*	*Ratio*	*Dates*	*Tons*	*Journeys*	*Ratio*
REFERENCE PHASES							
				1857-58	+	+	+
1858-60	+	+	+	1860-62	+	+	—
1862-66	+	+	—	1866-68	+	No data	No data
1868-73	+	No data	No data	1873-79	+	+	—
1879-83	+	+	+	1883-86	—	+	—
1886-90	+	+	+	1890-94	+	+	—
1894-1900	+	+	+	1900-01	—	+	—
1901-03	+	+	+	1903-04	+	+	+
1904-07	+	+	+	1907-08	—	+	—
PHASES IN TONS CONVEYED							
				1861-62	—	+	—
1862-67	+	+	—	1867-68	—	No data	No data
1868-73	+	No data	No data	1873-74	—	+	—
1874-77	+	+	—	1877-78	—	+	—
1878-83	+	+	+	1883-86	—	+	—
1886-91	+	+	+	1891-93	—	+	—
1893-1900	+	+	+	1900-01	—	+	—
1901-07	+	+	+	1907-08	—	+	—
1908-11	+	+	+	1911-12	—	No data	No data

Season ticket business more stable than other travel

About one-third of all journeys in Britain are authorized by season
tickets, good for a number of trips and sold at reduced rates. As far as
one can tell from annual figures for the years after World War I, sales
of season tickets did not actually rise and fall with the state of the
economy (Chart 8).[9] On the contrary, they declined continuously from
1920 to 1933; three business expansions failed to halt the downward
trend. But they did retard it. The number of tickets sold conformed, in
this sense, without exception from 1919 to 1938.

Apparently, however, this part of the passenger business was somewhat more stable, as far as cyclical disturbances are concerned, than

[9] Number of journeys on season tickets computed as explained in note 3.

TABLE 17
Journeys of Season Ticket Holders and Others, 1902-1913

	JOURNEYS OF OTHER PASSENGERS THAN SEASON TICKET HOLDERS (millions) (1)	NUMBER OF SEASON TICKETS[a] (thousands) (2)	JOURNEYS OF SEASON TICKET HOLDERS (2) x 600[a] (millions) (3)	TOTAL JOURNEYS (1) + (3) (4)	RATIO OF OTHER JOURNEYS TO TOTAL (1) ÷ (4) (5)
1902	1,188.2	592.6	355.6	1,543.8	.770
1903	1,195.3	618.0	370.8	1,566.1	.763
1904	1,198.8	643.9	386.3	1,585.1	.756
1905	1,199.0	663.0	397.8	1,596.8	.751
1906	1,240.3	693.5	416.1	1,656.4	.749
1907	1,259.5	715.6	429.4	1,688.9	.746
1908	1,278.1	721.8	433.1	1,711.2	.747
1909	1,265.1	730.3	438.2	1,703.3	.743
1910	1,306.7	752.7	451.6	1,758.3	.743
1911	1,326.3	779.2	467.5	1,793.8	.739
1912	1,294.3	785.1	471.1	1,765.4	.733
1913	1,454.8[b]	737.8[b]	442.7[b]	1,897.5	[b]

[a] Cf. note 3 to text.
[b] Not comparable with figures for other years: all journeys of workmen included in "other"; multiple-trip tickets for workmen formerly included in season tickets, and their journeys in those of season ticket holders.

the remainder; in other words, the number of individually purchased journeys tended to rise and fall by greater percentages than the number of journeys authorized by season tickets. The ratio of other-than-season-ticket journeys to all journeys rose in 4 of the 5 business expansions after 1918 for which we have data, fell in 4 of the 5 contractions (Chart 11). The fall in 1919-20 was not as rapid as in 1920-21; the rise in 1927-28 was slightly less rapid than that in 1928-29, considerably less rapid than in 1926-27.

The figures available for a short period before the war are harder to interpret. Rides of season ticket holders increased every year — did not, like other traffic, diminish from 1908 to 1909 or from 1911 to 1912 (Table 17). From their failure to do so we might infer greater stability. Although the ratio of non-season-ticket to total journeys fell in the three reference phases, the decline was more rapid in 1903-04 than in

CHART 11

Ratio of Journeys Other than Those of Season Ticket Holders to All Rail Journeys, 1919-1951

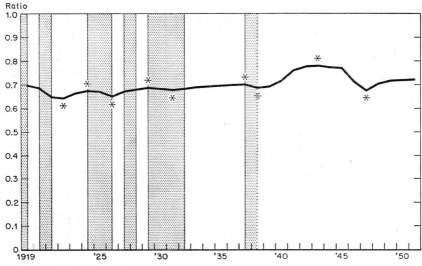

Shaded periods are reference contractions.

1904-07, as we should expect if other traffic is more variable. But in 1907-08 the ratio actually rose.[10]

[10] As we have noted before, perhaps we should regard the response of passenger traffic to business contraction as having occurred in 1908-1909. But even the 1908-1909 change, from .747 to .743 or —.004, differs negligibly from the average 1904-1907 change, (.756 — .746) ÷ 3 or — .0033, or the average 1904-1908 change, (.756 — .747) ÷ 4 or — .00225.

3. Use and Stocks of Equipment

More intensive use in prosperity

It has often been supposed that when the quantity of goods or services sold by a business enterprise increases, the managers of the enterprise ordinarily must increase their stock of equipment to cope with the growth of sales. In the railway industry, it might be supposed, an expansion of ton-miles requires an increase in the aggregate capacity of goods wagons (railway freight cars), an expansion of travel requires an increase in the capacity of carriages (railway passenger cars), and an expansion of total traffic cannot be handled without an increase in motive power. The supply of rolling stock, it is implied, will be adjusted to the level of traffic.

There are, of course, grounds for questioning whether these consequences must always or even usually occur. The supply of equipment at the beginning of a traffic expansion might be large enough to take care of the growth of traffic. It might be possible to use the initial equipment more efficiently. Even if railway managers feel that additional rolling stock is needed they may not be able to get it, for it takes time to build cars and locomotives, and they may not arrive from the construction shops until the boom is over. On the downswing, railway managers will certainly not reduce the stock of equipment in proportion to the fall in traffic. Perhaps they will junk some archaic or badly worn vehicles, but they will keep the rest, anticipating a return of prosperity, unless they think the decline in traffic is quasi-permanent and not merely cyclical.

In fact the changes in the supply of rolling stock have usually been much smaller than those in traffic, and have often been in the opposite direction. The size of the freight car stock ("wagon park") shows little positive relation to cycles in ton-miles. We have continuous figures on railroad-owned wagons only, although privately-owned rail wagons (mostly for coal) played an important part in freight movement; they were almost as numerous as those belonging to the railroads (Table 18).

TABLE 18

Privately-Owned and Railway-Owned Goods Wagons (Freight Cars)

PRIVATE[a]		RAILWAY[b]	
Aug. 1, 1918	628,344	Dec. 31, 1919	730,416
Aug. 1, 1928	638,215	Dec. 31, 1928	706,081
July 28, 1937	637,670	Dec. 31, 1937	656,834

[a] Dates are those of special censuses.

[b] Dates are most nearly comparable ones available. Figures include brake vans.

It does not seem likely, however, that the percentage changes in either stock during any phase of traffic was much greater than that in the other. At any rate, the railroad stock, although it grew in each expansion before World War I, never increased by as large a percentage as traffic; after the war it actually shrank (Table 19). Ton-miles per wagon in stock must have increased in every expansion. The number of wagons diminished in only two contractions, and then by a lesser percentage than traffic. The amount of traffic handled in a typical wagon during the course of a month must have diminished in every contraction.

TABLE 19

Freight Traffic and Number of Railway-Owned Wagons
Per Cent Change between Peak and Trough Years in Freight Traffic
1873-1908, 1921-1938

EXPANSIONS			CONTRACTIONS		
	Per cent change			Per cent change	
Dates	Traffic[a]	Wagons[b]	Dates	Traffic[a]	Wagons[b]
			1873-74	−1.3	6.1
1874-77	12.5	8.6	1877-78	−2.5	1.6
1878-83	28.9	15.0	1883-86	−4.4	10.9
1886-91	21.9	15.7	1891-93	−5.5	7.5
1893-1900	44.9	18.3	1900-01	−2.1	1.9
1901-07	24.0	5.5	1907-08	−4.7	1.0
1921-24	43.4	−5.1	1924-26	−26.3	0.6
1926-27	34.2	−0.2	1927-28	−5.9	−1.0
1928-29	6.3	−1.2	1929-32	−20.8	−4.0
1932-37	23.1	−2.6	1937-38	−9.3	2.1

[a] Tons conveyed, 1873-1908; net ton-miles 1921-38.

[b] Number of wagons for each year was computed by averaging numbers at beginning and end of that year. Percentage change was computed from these averages.

Railway coaches were more intensively used in years of large than in years of small travel. During expansions in travel for which we have data, the number of cars and their seating capacity either diminished, or increased by a smaller percentage than the number of passengers; in contractions, the fall in the number of travelers was always greater than the decline, if any, in the number of cars and seats; indeed the railroads actually increased the seating capacity a little in three such phases (Table 20).

TABLE **20**

Passenger Journeys, Number of Passenger Vehicles, and Number of Seats[a]
Per Cent Change between Peak and Trough Years in Journeys, 1920-1938

	EXPANSIONS				CONTRACTIONS		
	Per cent change				*Per cent change*		
	Jour-	*Ve-*			*Jour-*	*Ve-*	
Dates	*neys*[b]	*hicles*[c]	*Seats*[c]	*Dates*	*neys*[b]	*hicles*[c]	*Seats*[c]
				1920-22	−20.0	−1.0	1.3
1922-23	1.3	−1.2	−0.1	1923-26	−13.0	−0.5	3.7
1926-29[d]	10.6	1.1	2.5	1929-32	−8.7	−4.2	−1.4
				1929-32	−10.0	−5.0	−1.9
1932-37	13.5	−6.4	−3.7	1937-40	−25.3	−1.2	0.3

[a] Includes London underground railways, 1920-32; excludes them, 1929-38.
[b] Includes journeys of season ticket holders.
[c] Number for each year computed by averaging number at beginning and end of that year. Percentage change computed from these averages.
[d] Journeys, including London underground, did not contract in 1927-28.

We can't make direct comparisons between traffic and the number of locomotives; on the one hand, lacking data on passenger miles, we can't set up a composite measure of freight and passenger movement, and on the other, statistics on the stock of engines are not subdivided in accordance with the service to which engines were assigned. But the total number of steam locomotives declined almost continuously from 1920 to 1938 (Chart 18). Performance per locomotive must have increased when aggregate traffic was growing. The fall, if any, in the stock of engines during a contraction of travel or of ton-miles was always gradual. Between November 1929, a peak, and the second quarter of 1933, a trough in ton-miles, the number in stock declined from 23,497 (average for October, November, and December) to 21,454 (average for the quarter), a fall of 9 per cent. A similar computation for the somewhat different dates of the passenger contraction likewise yields a fall of 9 per cent. In all other contractions of freight or passenger traffic the number of locomotives declined 1 per cent or less.

Whenever traffic expanded, then, the railroads were able to handle more and more of it per car or locomotive on hand. Whenever it contracted, they got less and less remunerative work out of a typical unit of equipment. Rising traffic was accompanied by more intensive, and falling traffic by less intensive use. This can happen in either, or both, of two ways. The amount of work performed by an average car or locomotive during each hour of use may be higher in prosperity, because of heavier loading or faster movement; or vehicles may be kept in use during a greater percentage of the time, and spend fewer hours standing idle.

Heavier carloads and trainloads; but slower movement in freight service

In the movement of goods, the average weight loaded into a car increased and diminished with aggregate ton-miles (Chart 12).[1] These variations may reflect changes in the average weights to which the various kinds of traffic are loaded, or changes in the relative importance of heavily and lightly loaded species, or both. Data on loads are available for the three major subdivisions of ton-miles. They suggest that, in at least two instances, changes in composition must account for the fluctuation in the overall figure. In 1923-25, except at the very end, the average load of each component rose (general merchandise not conspicuously, but it did not decline either), yet the all-commodity average fell. In 1927-28, one component fell, then rose, one increased throughout, the third was steady, yet the average for all three declined continuously. In all other phases, however, changes in at least one of the components contributed to the characteristic change in the overall figure. Except at the coal strike troughs, the amplitude of the changes was rather small.[2]

From 1927 onward, marshalling yard staffs and others responsible for the make-up of trains were able to switch more and more loaded

---

[1] In discussing average loads and other operating statistics we rely on quarterly rather than monthly data after 1931, for reasons explained in the note on sources at the end of this paper.

[2] The sharp exceptional declines in the all-commodity averages resulted primarily from the virtual disappearance of the heavily-loaded coal traffic.

CHART 12

Average Wagon Load (Net Ton-miles per Loaded Wagon Mile) January 1920-First Quarter 1939

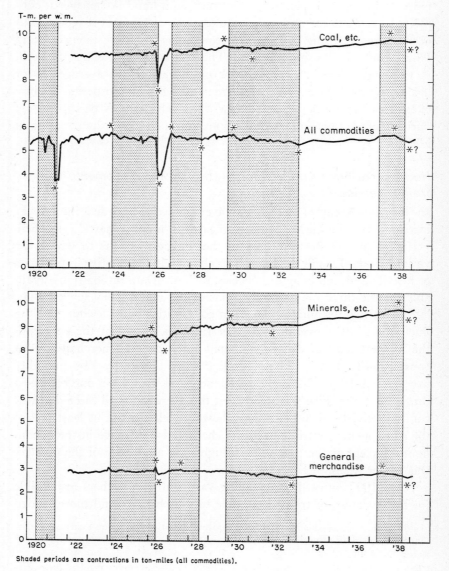

Shaded periods are contractions in ton-miles (all commodities).

cars into an average train as aggregate traffic swelled; when the latter diminished the average loaded length became shorter (Chart 13). In earlier phases the sequence of change was less regular. At the coal strike troughs, trains were lengthened enormously. Perhaps railway managers, confronted with a shortage of locomotive fuel, made unusual efforts, by lengthening trains, to get a maximum of work out of each engine.[3] Except near the trough, the change in 1920-21 and 1921-24 was normal by the standard of later cycles. The mild rise in the last half of 1921-24 did not persist; during most of the 1924-26 contraction the curve is flat, although it does not fall. The 1926-27 period violated the rule throughout; but coal production did not recover its normal level until near the end of this brief expansion (Chart 2).

Partly because of the changes in the average wagon-load and partly because of those in wagons per train, the average trainload became heavier in expansions and lighter in contractions of traffic (Chart 14). We can pair a cycle in ton-miles per train mile with each cycle in aggregate ton-miles. (At the 1921 and 1926 troughs the change in loaded length tended to counteract the effect on the average trainload of the change in tons per car, but the latter was more powerful.)

If the average speed of trains were constant, the cyclical variation in the trainload would mean that ton-miles per hour of train movement would increase in expansion and decrease in contraction. The labor of train crews would become more productive in the former and less productive in the latter. But in fact the movement of trains was, on the whole, accelerated in contraction and retarded in expansion, although the change was very irregular in 1924-26 and 1928-29 (Chart 15). Apparently greater density of traffic resulted in increased congestion and delay, and shrinkage of traffic permitted more freedom of movement. The changes in speed tended to counteract the effect of the changes in trainload on the work that could be accomplished in an hour. Indeed, there was no consistent relation between ton-miles per train-hour and aggregate volume (Chart 16).

Since there are no data on passenger-miles or passenger car-miles, we cannot compute passenger-miles per car-mile, car-miles per train-mile, or passenger-miles per train-mile. We can infer a good deal, however, about what happened to the last-mentioned ratio. Its numerator,

[3] Another possible surmise is that trains composed primarily of coal traffic are normally shorter than other trains and that the especially sharp cessation of this traffic therefore increased the average length.

CHART 13

Loaded Wagon Miles per Freight Train Mile, January 1920-First Quarter 1939

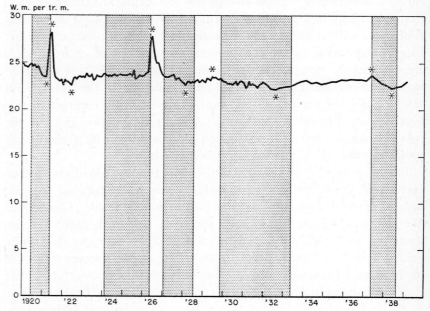

Shaded periods are contractions in ton-miles.

CHART 14

Average Train Load (Net Ton-miles per Freight Train Mile) January 1920-First Quarter 1939

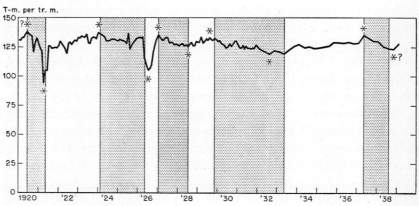

Shaded periods are contractions in ton-miles.

CHART 15

**Freight Train Miles per Freight Train Hour
January 1920-First Quarter 1939**

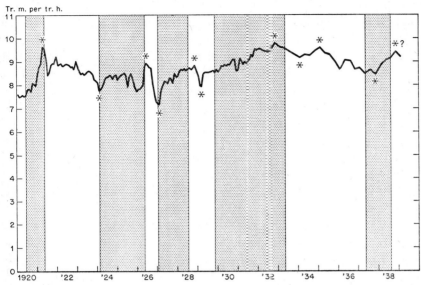

Shaded periods are contractions in ton-miles.

CHART 16

**Net Ton-miles per Freight Train Hour
January 1920-First Quarter 1939**

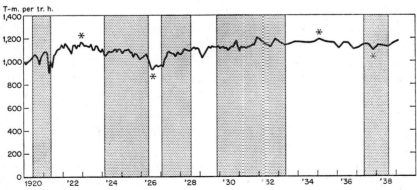

Shaded periods are contractions in ton-miles.

aggregate passenger-miles, is the arithmetical product of the average miles per journey and the number of journeys. It is not likely that the average length of journey increased in contractions of travel, which roughly coincided with contractions in business. On the contrary, as prosperity waned it is likely that people economized and took shorter journeys. Passenger-miles probably diminished by a greater percentage than the number of trips. Train-miles, on the other hand, diminished very little or actually increased (Chart 17). With passenger-miles falling and train-miles virtually constant or rising, passenger-miles per train-mile must have decreased — in other words, the average train-load fell.

In the first two expansions we must distinguish between the brief initial period of recovery from the strikes and the rest of the expansion. If we take the first three months after the strike effects had apparently subsided as a quasi-trough, we find, in 1921-24, that train-miles increased by a *greater* percentage than the number of passengers (Table 21, line 10). But this was not much of an expansion. Underground rides contracted during most of the time that rail journeys were expanding (Chart 9). In the combined totals that we are here obliged to examine (since train-miles cannot be segregated) there was no rise from one group of months to the next, except at the very end (Table 21, lines 6 to 10). From the 1927 quasi-trough to the 1930 peak, and likewise from 1933 to 1937, the number of journeys rose by a greater percentage than train-miles (lines 16 and 18). Since the average length of journey probably increased with prosperity, passenger-miles probably increased more than the number of trips and hence more than train-miles. We conclude that passenger train loads normally increase in expansions and decrease in contractions of travel. Patrons of the railroads would indeed be considerably inconvenienced if train service in contractions was reduced in proportion to traffic.

Matters went otherwise at the time of the strikes. In 1921, shortages of locomotive fuel eventually forced the railroads to curtail train service out of proportion to travel (lines 1 to 5). In 1926, when railroad workers participated in the earlier stages of the general strike, train service immediately fell off by a greater percentage than travel (lines 11 to 14).

The speed of passenger trains was not affected very much by cycles in travel (Chart 17). Again conditions were abnormal at the strike troughs. Probably, in an effort to serve both local and through traffic with a limited number of trains, the railroads greatly curtailed non-stop express service. Whatever the reasons, trains were slower than usual, and the miles-per-hour ratio shows a net rise in the expansions, a net fall in the contractions. But the change occurred principally in the immediate vicinity of the strikes, and the ratio would hardly have fluctuated in this way had there been no shortage of fuel for engines.

Passenger-miles per train-hour, a measure of the revenue-producing work performed by a train and its crew during a unit of time, is the arithmetical product of passenger-miles per train-mile and train-miles per train-hour — of the load and the speed. Since the load diminished in contractions, and the speed rose but little, we must conclude that passenger-miles per train-hour fell. Since the load increased and the speed also increased a little in expansions, hourly train performance increased. The productivity of passenger train crews, unlike that of freight train crews, goes up in expansions and down in contractions of traffic.[4]

Equipment used more of the time

Except at the coal strikes, the average load of freight cars did not change very much. The speed at which the cars travelled diminished in expansion and increased in contraction. Average hourly traffic performance, the product of the load and the speed, must have fallen in expansions and risen in contractions. The increase in performance per car in stock during expansions (Table 19) must have been achieved entirely by keeping cars loaded and in trains a greater percentage of the time. Likewise the fall in traffic performance per car in stock during contractions must be attributed entirely to a decline in the ratio of useful to total time.

The average number of passengers in a car no doubt increased and diminished with aggregate travel, and since there was little change in speed the average number of passenger-miles per hour of car movement must have increased and diminished similarly. But the larger number of train-miles at the peaks of travel suggests that a rise in the

[4] The equipment of British railways includes horses, road wagons, and motor trucks used in carting certain kinds of freight from consigners' business premises to railway stations and from stations to consignees' premises. Data on the average load per road wagon, the average load per truck, and the tonnage handled per working horse or truck per day, have been published, for two months of each year, usually February and September, 1922 to 1931, for one four-week period in 1932, and for another in 1933. They do not show any appreciable cyclical change.

TABLE 21

Rail Journeys and Coaching (i.e. Passenger) Train-Miles Selected Periods, 1921-1937

LINE	FIRST MONTH	LAST MONTH	NO. OF MONTHS	LEVEL OF NO. OF RAIL JOURNEYS	MONTHLY AVERAGE		% CHANGE FROM PRECEDING QUASI-TROUGH	
					No. of rail journeys	Train-miles[a] (millions)	No. of rail journeys	Train-miles
1	Jan. 1921	Mar. 1921	3	Quasi-trough	118.3	18.77	.....	-18
2	April 1921		1	Strike-depressed	94.2	15.48	-20	-45
3	May 1921		1	Strike-depressed	81.9	10.40	-31	-44
4	June 1921		1	Trough	77.7	10.54	-34	-15
5	July 1921		1	Strike-depressed	92.2	15.96	-22	.....
6	Aug. 1921	Oct. 1921	3	Quasi-trough	101.1	18.81	.....	.....
7	Nov. 1921	July 1922	9	Expansion	100.2	19.61	.....	.....
8	Aug. 1922	Apr. 1923	9	Expansion	100.2	20.42	.....	.....
9	May 1923	Jan. 1924	9	Expansion	100.4	20.76	.....	15
10	Feb. 1924	Apr. 1924	3	Peak	105.0	21.55	4	.....
11	Feb. 1926	Apr. 1926	3	Quasi-trough	103.4	22.03	.....	-55
12	May 1926		1	Trough	52.3	9.84	-49	-38
13	June 1926		1	Strike-depressed	71.3	13.56	-31	-21
14	July 1926		1	Strike-depressed	84.0	17.41	-19	.....
15	Jan. 1927	Mar. 1927	3	Quasi-trough	96.0	21.86	.....	7
16	Dec. 1929	Feb. 1930	3	Peak	104.3	23.49	9	.....
17	First quarter 1933		3	Trough	91.7	23.85	.....	9[b]
18	Second quarter 1937		3	Peak	122.5	25.99	34[b]	

[a] Rides on and train-miles of London underground railways are included.
[b] Per cent change from preceding actual trough.

CHART **17**

Passenger Train Miles and Train Speed
January 1920-First Quarter 1939

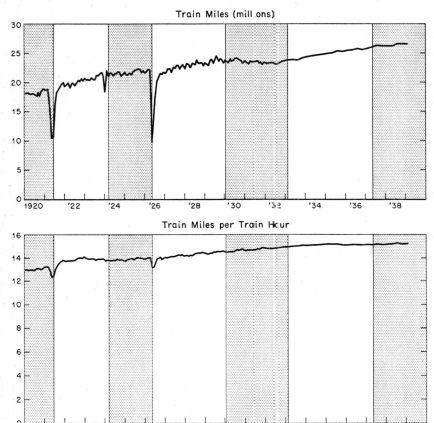

Train Miles (millions)

Train Miles per Train Hour

Shaded periods are contractions in number of rail journeys.
London underground railways included in all data.

percentage of time that cars were in operation contributed to the higher level of travel per car in stock.

As to motive power, we have direct figures on the average number of hours a locomotive spent in traffic per month (Chart 18). Although we cannot date the cycles in composite traffic exactly, the number of hours per month clearly rose in expansions and fell in contractions.

For the major kinds of equipment, then, the problem posed by expanding traffic was met in large part by running an existing stock of

CHART 18

**Steam Locomotives in Stock and
Hours in Traffic per Steam Locomotive per Month
May 1920-First Quarter 1939**

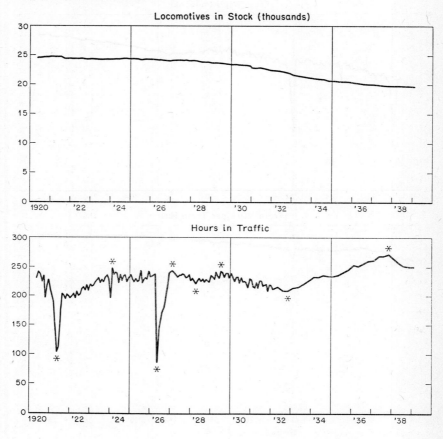

Locomotives in Stock (thousands)

Hours in Traffic

equipment for longer hours. At least this was the case in 1920-38, when a wave of traffic seldom overtopped its predecessor.

4. Maintenance Policy

When business activity falls off, wear and tear on plant and equipment diminishes. Managers of railways and of other business enterprises can reduce repair work to some extent without risking deterioration of their properties. Shortages of funds and impaired prospects of profit, however, may tempt them to cut repairs and replacements below the level required to keep plant and equipment in full-scale operating efficiency. Neglected properties may continue to function for a while, especially at depression levels of output. Conceivably, many enterprises might cut their maintenance work out of proportion to the reduction in the physical volume of their sales. Such a maintenance policy would tend to deepen the contraction in the national level of economic activity. Conversely, greater increases in maintenance than in sales would tend to accentuate booms in business.

Maintenance of track more stable than traffic

The history of British railroad way and works during World War II shows that maintenance can indeed be cut severely for a time without disrupting operations. To conserve resources for war construction and war industries, the railways were required greatly to reduce the quantities of ballast, cross-ties (sleepers), and rails they applied to their tracks (Chart 19). Maintenance policy in this period, however, was obviously governed by nonbusiness considerations. For information on the manner in which railway managers adjust their maintenance activities to cycles in traffic, we should confine our attention to the period ending in 1938.

Neither a train carrying goods nor a passenger train can run except over tracks in usable condition. Most of the tracks are used by both kinds of trains. In comparing changes in the quantities of track materials used with changes in traffic, we should employ some composite measure of the latter in which both classes of traffic would be repre-

51

sented. The statistical materials needed for a good measure are not available. We can safely assume, however, that from 1919 to 1938 the year-by-year *direction* of change in composite traffic was the same as in ton-miles.[1]

The *degree* of change in composite traffic is harder to estimate than the direction. If we had figures on passenger-miles, we would weight them and combine them with ton-miles. But we have only the number of journeys; for all we know, the average length of journeys may change appreciably during a business cycle, and if it does, the number is not a good measure. Lacking better data, we shall assume, where necessary, that a straight average of the percentage changes in ton-miles and number of passengers roughly approximates the change in composite traffic.

Changes in the quantities of materials used were at times irregular from year to year within an expansion or within a contraction of traffic. Applications of all three materials increased during the first, and diminished during the second year of the 1924-26 contraction. All three diminished during the first year of the 1932-37 expansion; sleepers and rails increased thereafter, ballast fluctuated a little from year to year without noticeable upward tendency.

The direction of net change over a whole expansion was more consistent. Application of each material at each peak was heavier than at the preceding trough.[2] In contraction there was no consistency. Ballast and rails declined in only 3 of 5 traffic contractions, sleepers in only 2.

But even if we found that the direction of change in materials was always the same as in traffic, a more interesting question, previously suggested, would remain to be answered. Were the changes in materials applied more violent than those in traffic?

The nature of the data is such that we must examine them in detail

[1] Except in 1921-22, 1923-24, and 1927-28, the number of passengers increased whenever ton-miles increased, and diminished whenever ton-miles diminished. From 1921 to 1922 ton-miles increased 26 per cent, while the number of journeys diminished only 2 per cent; a properly weighted composite measure would surely indicate an increase. From 1927 to 1928 ton-miles diminished 6 per cent, journeys increased only 1 per cent; a composite measure would show a decrease. Only the changes from 1923 to 1924 give trouble. Ton-miles increased 0.5 per cent, journeys fell 1.4 per cent. The peak year in ton-miles, 1924, may not have been a peak year for all kinds of traffic combined, but it was not far from being such a peak, and we shall so regard it.

[2] In 1932-37, however, the increase in ballast was negligible.

52

CHART 19

Material Used in Maintenance of Way and Works, 1919-1951

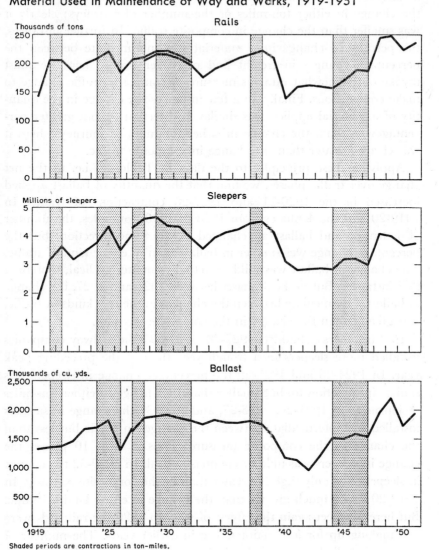

Shaded periods are contractions in ton-miles.

to answer this question. In the instances just noted, the railway companies applied more materials although their traffic declined. These, of course, are not instances of sharper decline in maintenance than of traffic; on the contrary, the policy followed was counter-cyclical in effect. In other instances, the change in maintenance, while similar in direction to the change in traffic, was smaller percentagewise than the change in either ton-miles or the number of journeys; clearly it was smaller than the change in composite traffic. In further instances, the percentage change in a material was intermediate between the percentage changes in freight and passenger traffic; here we must invoke our somewhat dubious measure of composite traffic change to make comparisons. Finally, in a few instances the change in the quantity of a material applied was similar in direction to, but greater percentagewise than, the change in either ton-miles or journeys; here it was clearly greater than the change in composite traffic.

Applying these principles to the data in Table 22, i.e. to the net change over traffic phases, we find that the quantity of ballast applied increased in the 1920-21 and 1927-28 contractions of traffic. In 1919-20 and the 4 phases from 1928 to 1938, ton-miles, the number of journeys, and ballast all changed in the same direction, but the percentage change was smaller in ballast than in either kind of traffic. The change in ballast was mild or actually counter-cyclical, therefore, in 7 instances. But in the 3 phases between 1921 and 1927, the change in ballast, intermediate between the changes in the two kinds of traffic, was greater than the change in the composite measure.

In 3 instances (1920-21, 1927-28, 1937-38) the railway companies installed more sleepers in a trough year than in the preceding peak year. In 1924-26 and 1928-29 the percentage change in sleepers was similar in direction to, but smaller than the change in either ton-miles or journeys. In 1921-24, 1926-27, and 1932-37 the change in sleepers installed was intermediate between the changes in traffic but less than the change in the composite measure. Thus in 8 of 10 phases the change in sleepers was mild or counter-cyclical. In 1929-32 the change in sleepers was only slightly greater than in the composite measure. In 1919-20 it was much greater than the change in either kind of traffic. But here we meet again the effects of war. In 1920 the railroads were still making up for low maintenance in earlier years. The number of sleepers installed is especially likely to decline in wartime because Britain must rely so heavily on imports for timber.

The tonnage of rails laid increased in the 1927-28 and 1937-38 contractions of traffic. In 1920-21, 1929-32, and 1932-37 the changes in ton-miles, journeys, and rails were similar in direction but the per-

TABLE 22

Traffic and Materials Used in Maintenance of Track
Per Cent Change between Years of Peaks and Troughs in Ton-Miles, 1919-1938

DATE	LEVEL OF TON-MILES	NET TON-MILES		PASSENGER JOURNEYS		COMPOSITE TRAFFIC	BALLAST		SLEEPERS		RAILS	
		Billions	% Change	Millions	% Change	% Change	Thous. cu. yds.	% Change	Thousands	% Change	Thous. tons	% Change
1919	Trough	......	......	2,065	......	......	1,323	......	1,793	......	142.2	......
1920	Peak	19,173	4.3[a]	2,186	5.9	5.1	1,346	1.7	3,172	76.9	205.2	44.3
1921	Trough	13,289	-30.7	1,787	-18.3	-24.5	1,365	1.4	3,614	13.9	204.9	-.1
1924	Peak	19,063	43.4	1,747	-2.2	20.6	1,686	23.5	3,773	4.4	207.9	1.5
1926	Trough	14,042	-26.3	1,542	-11.7	-19.0	1,300	-22.9	3,508	-7.0	183.2	-11.9
1927	Peak	18,847	34.2	1,651	7.1	20.6	1,667	28.2	4,064	15.8	206.7	12.8
1927	Peak	18,817	......	1,651	......	......	1,045	......	4,298	......	205.6	......
1928	Trough	17,733	-5.9	1,666	.9	-2.5	1,858	12.9	4,590	6.8	209.3	1.8
1929	Peak	18,855	6.3	1,705	2.3	4.3	1,891	1.8	4,648	1.3	219.9	5.1
1932	Trough	14,942	-20.8	1,557	-8.7	-14.8	1,814	-4.1	3,911	-15.9	201.4	-8.4
1932	Trough	14,933	......	1,141	......	......	1,807	......	3,873	......	195.8	......
1937	Peak	18,384	23.1	1,295	13.5	18.3	1,808	.1	4,428	14.3	215.0	9.8
1938	Trough	16,672	-9.3	1,236	-4.6	-7.0	1,751	-3.2	4,496	1.5	221.6	3.1

[a] Per cent change in tons originated. Computed from Table 1.

centage change in rails was smallest. In the 3 phases between 1921 and 1927, the change in rails was intermediate between the traffic changes but much less than their average. On the other hand, tonnage laid increased a little more than the composite traffic measure in 1928-29, and much more than either component of traffic (although much less than sleepers) in 1919-20. Steel had been diverted from the railways to the war effort before 1919; in 1920 they were still making the deficit good.

On the whole, maintenance of track was more stable than traffic in the interwar period. Cyclical fluctuations in traffic were certainly not regularly accompanied by similar but more violent fluctuations in quantities of track material installed.

Traffic and maintenance of rolling stock equally variable

From 1920 to 1938 the British railways reported the number of vehicles charged to capital account, the number of renewals, and the number of heavy and light repairs. Whether a vehicle is charged to capital or included in renewals depends on whether it is regarded as a net addition to the stock or as a replacement. A "renewal" is not necessarily a rebuilt unit; it may be a newly built unit. Equipment stocks were stable or declining in these years, and vehicles charged to capital account were sometimes negligible in number, always much fewer than renewals. The impact on the national economy of an increase or decrease in equipment work is much the same, however the railway accountants classify the work. We have combined the two kinds of figures under the heading of gross additions.[3]

Locomotives, passenger cars excluding rail motor vehicles, and goods wagons were the three most important objects of equipment maintenance expense. Changes in the supply and condition of passenger cars can be compared with cycles in passenger traffic, and changes in

[3] The classification was changed in 1927. Figures are available for that year on both the old and the new basis. The category of heavy repairs to wagons was seriously affected, since the number dropped from 121,276 to 69,583. Other categories were less seriously affected.

The old classification subdivided wagon renewals into those "on complete renewal account" and those "on partial renewal account." The latter were comparatively few, ranging from 6,281 in 1924 to none in 1927. We use only the "complete renewal" figures.

The London and North Eastern included 175 passenger carriages in suspense account in 1936 but transferred them to capital account in 1937. We include them in our 1936 figure for "additions."

wagons with cycles in freight traffic. Data on locomotives (which were not and probably could not be subdivided by branch of service) may be compared with data on engine miles.[4]

During a long expansion or contraction of traffic, the course of gross additions or repairs to equipment, like that of track materials applied, was sometimes far from smooth (Charts 20, 21, 22). Additions to the supply of carriages, for example, were somewhat fewer in 1933 than in 1932; they increased rapidly in the next three years, then fell off abruptly from 1936 to 1937. Heavy repairs to locomotives fluctuated irregularly in 1921-25.

But the railway companies usually added more vehicles to their stock and made more repairs in a year of peak traffic than in the preceding or following trough year. Column (5) in Table 23 shows the number of traffic phases in which the direction of net change in additions or repairs was the same as the direction of change in traffic, and column (6) the number of phases in which the direction was different. In 8 of the 9 categories of additions or repairs, similarities outnumbered differences. The exception — light repairs to locomotives — is one of the categories for which we have comparatively few observations. When all observations for all categories in all expansions and contractions are totaled, we find 57 instances of similar and only 12 of dissimilar change.

But we have yet to determine how often the changes in additions and repairs were large in comparison with the changes in traffic. The requisite data appear in Table 24 and are summarized in Table 25. The number of phases in which the direction of net change in equipment-traffic ratios agreed with the direction of change in traffic itself is shown in column (5) and the number of disagreements in column (6). For most of the 9 categories the observations divide fairly evenly. Instances of agreement outnumbered instances of disagreement in only 2 categories. When observations on all categories in all traffic phases are totaled, we find 32 instances of agreement and 37 of disagreement. The additions-traffic and repairs-traffic ratios did not consistently rise when traffic was growing and fall when it was diminishing. Cyclical

[4] Maintenance charges on rail motor vehicles were very small, and the use of these vehicles was confined to a minor part of the rail network. We therefore disregard them. Additions and repairs of "other coaching vehicles" (for baggage, mail, parcels traffic, etc.) were a good deal less numerous than in the case of passenger cars; in the absence of a good measure of the traffic that uses them, we disregard them also.

TABLE **23**

Gross Additions and Repairs to Equipment
Number of Net Rises and Net Falls during Expansions and
during Contractions in Traffic, 1919-1938

| | IN EXPANSIONS | | IN CONTRACTIONS | | TOTALS | | |
| | *Rises* | *Falls* | *Rises* | *Falls* | *(1)+(4)* | *(2)+(3)* | *(5)+(6)* |
	(1)	(2)	(3)	(4)	(5)	(6)	(7)
Locomotives:							
Additions	4	1	1	4	8	2	10
Heavy repairs	5	0	0	5	10	0	10
Light repairs	0	2*	1	2	2	3	5
Carriages:							
Additions	4	0	2	2	6	2	8
Heavy repairs	3	1	0	4	7	1	8
Light repairs	1	0	1	1	2	1	3
Wagons:							
Additions	4	1	0	5	9	1	10
Heavy repairs	3	2	0	5	8	2	10
Light repairs	2	0	0	3	5	0	5
Total	26	7	5	31	57	12	69

Derived from charts 20, 21, and 22. For example, more locomotives were added to
the stock in 1920 than in 1919, in 1925 than in 1921, in 1927 than in 1926, in 1937
than in 1932 — 4 expansions in all. Fewer were added in 1929 than in 1928 — the
only instance of decline in expansion. We enter 4 in col. (1) and 1 in col. (2). The
procedure for contractions is similar. For each kind of equipment, the dates compared are those of peaks and troughs in the appropriate kind of traffic, as indicated
on the charts.

Although there are no traffic data for 1914-18, we assume that all kinds of traffic
were at a trough in 1919, i.e. were lower than in 1918. Although engine miles were
lower in 1939 than in 1938, aggregate hours worked by engines were higher; hours
and miles agree in direction of change in all other years; we assume 1938 was a
trough in use of engines. Although passenger traffic declined from 1937 to 1940 we
assume that the decline after 1938 was connected with unusual conditions imposed
by war and that for business-cycle purposes 1938 may be regarded as a trough.
* Includes one instance of no change (1932-37).

swings in additions and repair work were not consistently greater than
swings in traffic; nor were they consistently smaller.[5]

[5] It is possible, of course, that fluctuations in traffic did tend to induce dispropor-
tionately large changes in additions and repairs, but that their influence was obscured
by the influence of other factors. The presence of such a suppressed tendency would
be suggested if (a) the additions-traffic and repairs-traffic ratios, when they rose in
a traffic contraction, nevertheless rose less rapidly than in the preceding or following
expansion, and if (b) the ratios, when they fell in an expansion, nevertheless fell
more rapidly in the preceding or following contraction. We made some calculations
in accordance with this more subtle test, but they yielded no evidence that fluctuations in the number of additions and repairs tend to be consistently more violent (or
consistently less violent) than fluctuations in traffic. We shall not burden the reader
with them.

CHART **20**

Additions and Repairs to Stock of Locomotives, 1919-1938

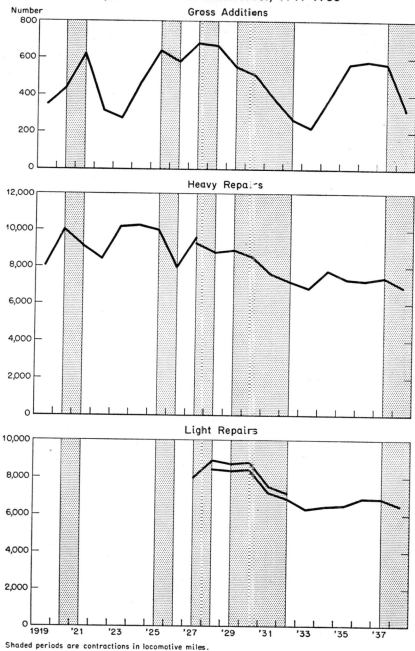

Number

Gross Additions

Heavy Repairs

Light Repairs

Shaded periods are contractions in locomotive miles.

CHART **21**

Additions and Repairs to Stock of Passenger Cars, 1919-1938

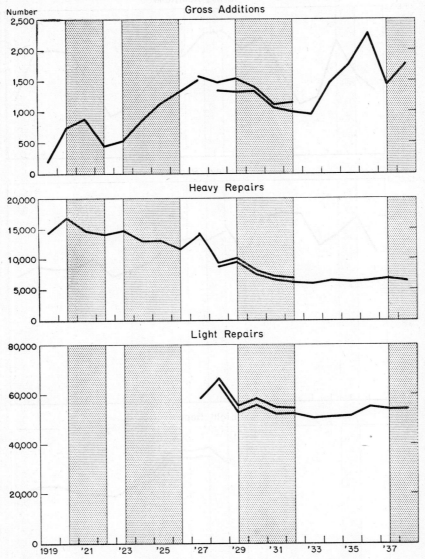

Shaded periods are contractions in number of journeys (including those of season ticket holders).

CHART 22

Additions and Repairs to Stock of Goods Wagons, 1919-1938

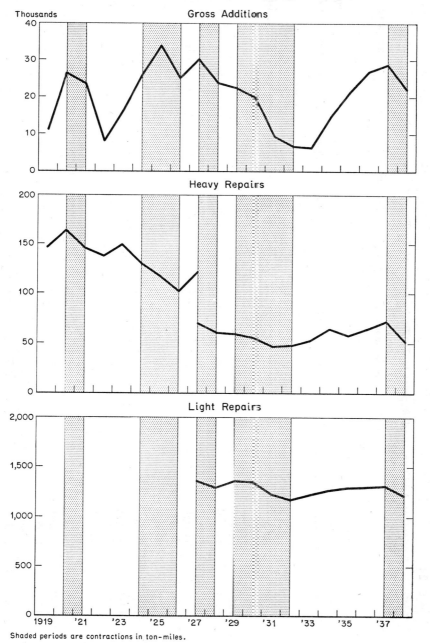

Gross Additions

Heavy Repairs

Light Repairs

Shaded periods are contractions in ton-miles.

TABLE **24**

Ratios of Equipment Additions and Repairs to Traffic in Years of Traffic Peaks and Troughs, 1919-1938

DATE	LEVEL OF TRAFFIC[a]	YEARS FROM PRECEDING DATE	GROSS ADDITIONS[b]		HEAVY REPAIRS		LIGHT REPAIRS[e]	
			Number	Total change	Number	Total change	Number	Total Change
					LOCOMOTIVES, PER MILLION ENGINE MILES			
1919	Trough	....	.677	......	15.73	......		
1920	Peak	1	.783	.106	18.02	2.29		
1921	Trough	1	1.330	.547	19.58	1.56		
1925	Peak	4	1.082	−.248	16.92	−2.66		
1926	Trough	1	1.158	.076	15.89	−1.03		
1927	Peak	1	1.126	−.032	15.85[d]	−0.04	13.21	......
1928	Trough	1	1.112	−.014	14.62	−0.76	14.78	1.57
1929	Peak	1	.902	−.210	14.43	−0.19	14.22	−0.56
1932	Trough	3	.482	−.420	12.77	−1.66	12.71	−1.51
1929[c]	Peak	....	.944	......	15.07	......	14.23	......
1932	Trough	3	.508	−.436	13.44	−1.63	12.86	−1.37
1937	Peak	5	.948	.440	12.39	−1.05	11.48	−1.38
1938	Trough	1	.539	−.409	11.73	−0.66	11.04	−0.44
					PASSENGER CARRIAGES, PER MILLION PASSENGER JOURNEYS[f]			
1919	Trough	....	.095	......	6.95	......		
1920	Peak	1	.342	.247	7.72	0.77		
1922	Trough	2	.252	−.090	8.06	0.34		
1923	Peak	1	.296	.044	8.28	0.22		

62

1926	Trough	3	.850^g	.554	7.55^h	−0.73		
1929	Peak	3	.901	.017	5.91	−1.72	32.4	......
1932	Trough	3	.737	−.164	4.42	−1.49	34.9	2.5
1929^e	Peak	....	1.040	......	7.55	......	41.6	......
1932	Trough	3	.872	−.168	5.44	−2.11	45.6	4.0
1937	Peak	5	1.111	.239	5.27	−0.17	41.5	−4.1
1938	Trough	1	1.440	.329	5.21	−0.06	43.6	2.1

WAGONS, PER MILLION NET TON-MILES^i

1920	Peak	....	1.492	......	8.50	......		
1921	Trough	1	1.800	.308	10.97	2.47		
1924	Peak	3	1.459	−.341	6.86	−4.11		
1926	Trough	2	1.803	.344	7.28	0.42		
1927	Peak	1	1.608	−.195	6.13	−0.85		
1927	Peak	....	1.608	......	3.69	......	72.52	......
1928^{ej}	Trough	1	1.346	−.262	3.40	−0.29	73.23	0.71
1929	Peak	1	1.193	−.153	3.14	−0.26	72.36	−0.87
1932	Trough	3	.463	−.730	3.21	0.07	78.76	6.40
1937	Peak	5	1.983	1.520	3.93	0.72	71.47	−7.29
1938	Trough	1	1.618	−.365	3.09	−0.84	72.64	1.17

^{a} Measured by engine-miles, number of journeys, and ton-miles, as appropriate.

^{b} Total of vehicles charged to capital account and to renewals account. Excludes wagons on partial renewal account (none reported after 1926. No such category after 1927).

^{c} Not reported, 1919-26.

^{d} 15.38 for comparison with later years.

^{e} Railways later taken over by London Passenger Transport Board included above, not included on this line or below.

^{f} Including estimated journeys of season ticket-holders.

^{g} .884 for comparison with later years. Ratio of locomotives charged to capital account plus renewals, new basis, 1927 to same, old basis, 1927 = 1.0396; 1.04 × .850 = .884.

^{h} 7.63 for comparison with later years. Ratio of heavy repairs, new basis, 1927 to same, old basis, 1927 = 1.0104; 1.01 × 7.55 = 7.63.

^{i} Including free-hauled and livestock.

^{j} Figures including and excluding LPTB practically same 1928-32.

TABLE 25

Ratios of Equipment Gross Additions and Repairs to Traffic
Number of Net Rises and Net Falls during Expansions and
during Contractions in Traffic, 1919-1938

KIND OF EQUIPMENT AND NUMERATOR OF RATIO	IN EXPANSIONS		IN CONTRACTIONS		TOTALS		
	Rises (1)	*Falls* (2)	*Rises* (3)	*Falls* (4)	$\overline{(1)+(4)}$ (5)	(2)+(3) (6)	(5)+(6) (7)
Locomotives:							
Additions[a]	2	3	2	3	5	5	10
Heavy repairs[a]	1	4	1	4	5	5	10
Light repairs[a]	0	2	1	2	2	3	5
Carriages:							
Additions[b]	4	0	2	2	6	2	8
Heavy repairs[b]	2	2	1	3	5	3	8
Light repairs[b]	0	1	2	0	0	3	3
Wagons:							
Additions[c]	2[d]	3	2	3	5	5	10
Heavy repairs[c]	2[d]	3	3	2	4	6	10
Light repairs[c]	0	2	3	0	0	5	5
Total	13	20	17	19	32	37	69

[a] Denominator, millions of engine-miles.
[b] Denominator, millions of passengers.
[c] Denominator, millions of net ton-miles.
[d] Includes a rise, from 1919 to 1920, in additions or repairs per million tons origi-nated; ton-miles not available.
Derived from Table 24.

Fluctuations in traffic, then, are not usually translated in exagger-ated form into fluctuations in maintenance either of track or of equip-ment. Maintenance of track is somewhat more stable than traffic, maintenance of equipment does not differ appreciably from traffic in amplitude of fluctuation. Track is more vulnerable to the weather than equipment. A large amount of work must be done to keep it usable, whether it is lightly or heavily used. Other components in way and works — ditches, embankments, poles and wires, buildings and bridges — may be similarly vulnerable.

5. Use of Labor and Fuel

In discussions of business cycles and their causes the opinion has some-times been expressed that costs rise near the end of expansions. In part the supposed rise is attributed to a decline in efficiency: more labor and materials are required per unit of product. Conversely, cost is supposed to fall and the use of labor and materials to become more economical toward the end of contraction. It is thought that the changes in cost help to bring on the downturn and the upturn in business by their effects on prices and profits. Others contend that the large scale of operations near a business peak is necessarily associated with low costs and urge that prices and wage rates be set with the asso-ciation in mind. We can extract some information on these matters from the British railway data, although the units of time to which the figures pertain are not short enough to reveal all the relevant changes that may occur.

Unit labor requirements inversely related to traffic

Labor expense on British railways is more closely related to the num-ber of workers than to the number of manhours worked. Men available for work throughout a week are guaranteed a full standard week's wages if they are employed at all.[1] When traffic increases, management can keep the men already on the payroll busier at no extra cost. If the number of men on the payroll does not rise in proportion to traffic during an expansion, labor cost per traffic unit will tend to decline. If the number of workers does not diminish in proportion to traffic during

[1] *Ministry of Labour Gazette,* April 1919, p. 125. *Railway Gazette,* November 10, 1922, p. 595; June 2, 1923, p. 828; March 13, 1931, p. 422; March 20, 1931, p. 466. Ministry of Labour and National Service, *Time Rates of Payment and Hours of Labour,* September, 1948, pp. 42, 130.

a contraction, unit labor cost will tend to rise.[2] And apparently the number of workers usually did not rise or fall as much as traffic (Table 26).

The foregoing remarks pertain strictly to work done during standard working hours. Overtime, and night and Sunday work (at least where they are not included in a man's regularly assigned hours) are paid for more nearly in proportion to the hours worked. Furthermore, the number of such hours tends to increase and decrease out of proportion to traffic. Aggregate payments for extra time, however, must be small in comparison with those for straight time.

In addition to the evidence of Table 26, we have more specific information on the relation between labor input and traffic for certain occupations. In an earlier chapter we found that the average load of freight trains tends to vary directly with traffic, but that the gain in hourly performance which might be expected from the increase in load is largely dissipated by decline in speed. As far as labor cost is concerned, however, the decline in speed will often have no importance. A train crew might, for example, have a daily run that required 6 hours at the beginning of an expansion and 7 hours at the end. They would be entitled to 8 hours' pay in either case, and it might not be feasible to assign them other tasks in the left-over time. Since their train will carry a heavier load, the labor cost per ton-mile will be lower at the end. In passenger traffic, we found, fluctuations in traffic do not affect speed. Since there are more passengers in a train during prosperity, train labor costs per passenger-mile must be lower than in depression.

If a run is longer than 140 miles, the train crew receives an extra hour's pay (i.e. the weekly rate divided by the number of hours in a full-time week) for each additional 15 miles. But in such instances too, the pay is the same regardless of the tonnage or number of passengers carried; growth of traffic does not affect the length of runs, which is fixed by the location of terminals.

Many workers in railways shops are paid by the piece rather than by the week. Unless the number of "pieces" paid for fluctuates more than traffic, expenses for this kind of work will normally be constant per traffic unit. But labor agreements apparently provide that the

---

[2] These tendencies may, of course, be offset by countervailing changes in full-time weekly hours or in weekly rates of pay.

TABLE 26

Ton-miles, Journeys, and Employees, at Peaks and Troughs in First Quarter Ton-miles, 1921-1939

DATE (QUARTER ENDED MARCH 31)	LEVEL OF TON-MILES[a]	TON-MILES		JOURNEYS		TRAFFIC	EMPLOYEES	
		Amount (millions)	% change from preceding date	Number (millions)	% change from preceding date	% change from preceding date[b]	Number (thousands)	% change from preceding date
1921	Trough	3,989	.....	325.5	.....	.....	736	.....
1924	Peak	4,933	23.7	277.6	−14.7	4.5	701	−4.8
1925	Trough	4,795	−2.8	280.6	1.1	−0.8	702	0.1
1927	Peak	4,968	3.6	265.6	−5.3	−0.8	683	−2.7
1928	Trough	4,621	−7.0	277.9	4.6	−1.2	677	−0.9
1930	Peak	4,776	3.4	288.5	3.8	3.6	657	−3.0
1933	Trough	3,856	−19.3	254.9	−11.6	−15.4	566	−13.9
1938	Peak	4,753	23.3	294.1	15.4	19.4	607	7.2
1939	Trough	4,457	−6.2	285.2	−3.0	−4.6	589	−3.0

[a] As determined from first-quarter data, 1920-39, ignoring data for other quarters.

[b] Straight average of percentages for ton-miles and passengers. The data on ton-miles and journeys pertain to the first three months of each year. Those on employees (published in Ministry of Transport, *Railway Returns, Staff*, annual) were obtained in a census of railway employment taken in a week ending in March each year, except that the 1927 Census was taken in the week ended April 30. For other years the ending day ranges from March 7 to March 29. There was no census before 1921. The data in this table are not seasonally adjusted. All include the rail traffic or employment of the LPTB or its predecessors.

earnings of piece workers shall not fall below a weekly minimum.[3] If the number of pieces furnished to each man becomes so small that this provision comes into play, further declines in the number of pieces will be accompanied by rising cost per piece.

Although the nature of the rules governing wages is such that the ratio of man-hours to traffic is unimportant for the study of costs, that ratio is interesting from other points of view, and the lack of information on man-hours is therefore regrettable. We do have a little information about hourly productivity in one kind of work — the assembling of wagons into trains. It is performed in marshalling yards, in which a track is assigned to each destination or group of destinations for which a train is to be formed, and each wagon to be forwarded is shunted to the appropriate track. The number of cars handled per man-hour in such yards tended to rise and fall with aggregate ton-miles (Chart 23). If we could divide ton-miles, rather than wagons marshalled, by man-hours of this kind of labor, we would probably find that ton-miles also fluctuated more than hours worked in shunting — in other words that the marshalling labor required per ton-mile tends to fall in expansions and rise in contractions.[4]

Fuel economy related to cycles in volume

Cyclical growth of traffic apparently results in a less than proportionate increase in fuel burned by locomotives, and cyclical decline of traffic in a less than proportionate reduction of fuel requirements. A curve depicting ton-miles per pound of coal consumed in freight ser-

[3] Last reference, note 1. See also *Railway Gazette,* August 4, 1922, p. 151.

[4] Incoming trains, the wagons in which have reached a parting of the ways to their ultimate destination, supply part of the cars to be marshalled; others are picked up locally and brought to the yard. Both are included in the numerator of the ratio charted. The denominator comprises man-hours of "Yard Masters, Assistant Yard Masters, Yard Inspectors, Yard Foremen, Leading Shunters, Shunters, Capstan Foremen, Capstanmen, and Goods Pointsmen." From 1922 to 1931 the data cover work in February (March in 1924) and August. We average the two figures for each year and plot them midway between the two months. Only a February sample was taken in 1926; since the seasonal appears large in comparison with the cyclical variation we do not show a figure for that year. From 1932 to 1938 the data cover operations during a four-week period ending early in October. The number of yards included, 1922-38, ranges from 109 to 124.

Data on man-hours spent in loading small shipments into and out of cars, per ton of goods handled, are likewise available for occasional months or four-week periods, 1922-38. They indicate little if any cyclical variation in unit labor requirements for this kind of work.

CHART **23**

Ton-miles, and Wagons Detached in Marshaling Yards
per Man-hour of Shunting Staff Labor, Various Dates

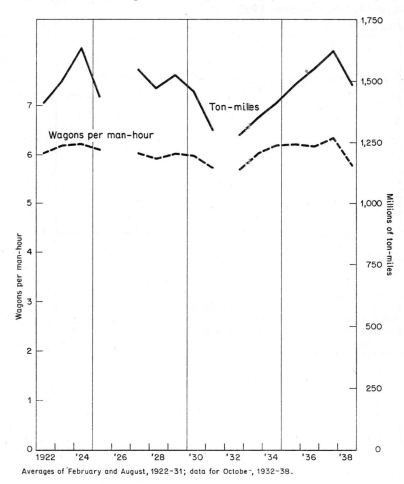

Averages of February and August, 1922-31; data for October, 1932-38.

vice since 1921 is highly irregular, but we think we discern an upward
drift in every expansion, a downward drift in all contractions except,
perhaps, 1926-27 (Chart 24).[5]

[5] *Railway Statistics* reports coal consumption per steam locomotive mile in freight
service. Consumption and mileage of locomotives assigned to shunting freight were
excluded from the computation 1921-35, included 1935-39 (overlaps in 1935). Con-
(Continued on page 70)

CHART **24**

Net Ton-miles per Pound of Coal Consumed by Steam Locomotives in Freight Service
August 1921-First Quarter 1939

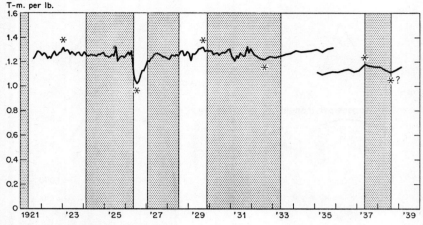

Shaded periods are contractions in ton-miles.
Coal consumed in shunting freight not included in divisor 1921-35, included 1935-39.

sumption and mileage of engines in departmental work (hauling work trains, etc.) and road engines engaged in incidental shunting are included throughout. We multiplied the average per mile by the corresponding kinds of locomotive mileage to find aggregate consumption, which we then divided into ton-miles. Since coal used in shunting service is included in the divisor for the 1935-39 segment of the curve, the level of that segment is lower than the level for 1921-35.

6. Financial Returns

Expense ratio and unit cost varied inversely with traffic

From 1919 to 1938, an expansion of traffic usually brought with it a greater percentage increase in railway operating revenues than in railway operating expenses; a contraction of traffic was accompanied by a greater percentage shrinkage of revenues than of expenses. The ratio of railway expenditures to railway gross receipts, usually called the operating ratio, generally declined, and the ratio of net receipts to gross receipts rose in expansion; the operating ratio rose, and the margin of profit declined, in contraction (Chart 25). There were exceptions in 1919-20 and 1927-28.[1]

The operating ratio equals the average expense per unit of traffic, divided by the average revenue per unit of traffic. Unit expense therefore equals the product of unit revenue and the operating ratio.[2] We know what happened to the operating ratio; if we can learn what hap-

---

[1] For reasons advanced in an earlier section, we assume that in 1920-38 the expansions and contractions in a composite measure of all railway traffic would correspond to those in ton-miles. Since the operating ratio is available for many earlier years, we thought of investigating its relation to cycles in traffic during a long period before World War I. But when we look at the traffic figures for that period, we find that passenger traffic hardly ever changed in the same direction as freight traffic except when both were expanding. During every contraction in tons conveyed, the number of journeys increased; during every contraction in journeys, tonnage increased. There was only one exception; both contracted from 1911 to 1912. In all other years of opposite change, moreover, the kind of traffic that happened to be growing would likely preponderate over the other kind in any reasonably constructed index of composite traffic, except perhaps in 1867-68, 1891-93, and 1907-1908. As far as we can tell, there were few if any cycles (comparable in length to business cycles) in total traffic. Instead there was almost continuous growth.

We did compare changes in the operating ratio during *business* expansions with those during business contractions, but found no systematic variation.

[2] In formulating these equations we assume that the many varieties of traffic are somehow combined in a single measure. The equations are valid, however, whatever the measure employed. In any case, revenue ÷ expense = revenue per unit × traffic ÷ expense per unit × traffic = revenue per unit ÷ expense per unit. But in studying cyclical relations between prices received and costs it would be desirable

(Continued on page 72)

71

pened to the unit revenue we will also know what happened to unit cost. The observed fluctuations in the operating ratio may mean that the average cost of handling traffic usually rises when traffic shrinks and falls when traffic grows. To determine whether they really have this meaning we must examine them in the light of the history of rates and fares in 1919-38.

During the 1914-18 war, when the railways were operated on lease to and for the account of the government, freight rates were kept stable, and remained at their prewar level in 1919. But rising wage-rates and prices of railway material, together with the prospect of return to private financial responsibility, led the Minister of Transport to approve general increases in 1920. On January 15 rates on coal, coke, and patent fuel were advanced to 25 per cent above prewar. Rates on commodities in the lettered classes A, B, and C (i.e. commodities of low value per ton, shipped in large quantities) were raised to 30, 40, and 50 per cent respectively. Those on articles in the numbered classes (1 to 5) were raised to 60 per cent. On top of these percentage increases, flat rates per ton were imposed ranging from 3 pence on the less valuable to 12 pence on the more valuable commodities. On September 1 all freight rates were raised to 100 per cent above prewar. Passenger fares (other than workmen's fares and the prices of season tickets) which had been raised to 50 per cent on January 1,

---

to measure composite traffic in such a way that revenue per traffic unit would be influenced exclusively by changes in rates and fares (not by changes in the composition of traffic). Although we cannot construct such measures of traffic and of unit revenue, it may be illuminating to consider what they would be like if we could.

Each kind of traffic to which a distinct rate applies should be considered a distinct species. For comparing a base year, I (such as a peak or trough), with a later year, II, the traffic in each species (measured in whatever unit the railroads use in quoting rates on that species, e.g. the cwt.) could be weighted in each year by the rate applicable to it in the base year. Thus t_{a1} units of species A, carried in I at a rate of r_{a1} per unit would be counted as $t_{a1} \, r_{a1}$ *traffic* units, t_{b1} units of B in I at r_{b1} as $t_{b1} \, r_{b1}$ traffic units, and so on for all other species. Aggregate traffic in I would be $t_{a1} \, r_{a1} + t_{b1} \, r_{b1} + \cdots$, or $\Sigma \, t_1 r_1$. It would be identical with aggregate revenue in I. Aggregate traffic in II would be $t_{a2} \, r_{a1} + t_{b2} \, r_{b1} + \cdots$, or $\Sigma \, t_2 \, r_1$. It would *not* usually be identical with revenue in II.

Revenue per unit in I would be 1. Revenue per unit in II would be $\Sigma \, t_2 r_2 \div \Sigma \, t_2 r_1$. Only changes in rates and fares could cause it to differ from 1.

These formulae conform to the rule that expense ratio = unit cost ÷ unit revenue. Let E_1 and E_2 be aggregate expense in the respective years. Then in year I, operating ratio = $E_1/\Sigma t_1 r_1 \div 1$ = unit cost ÷ unit revenue, and in II, operating ratio = $E_2/\Sigma t_2 r_2 = E_2/\Sigma t_2 r_1 \times \Sigma t_2 r_1/\Sigma t_2 r_2 = E_2/\Sigma t_2 r_1 \div \Sigma t_2 r_2/\Sigma t_2 r_1$ = unit cost ÷ unit revenue. Furthermore,

$$\frac{\text{unit cost in II}}{\text{unit cost in I}} = \frac{\text{operating ratio in II}}{\text{operating ratio in I}} \cdot \frac{\text{unit revenue in II}}{\text{unit revenue in I}}$$

CHART 25

Ratio of Railway Expenditures and of Net Revenue to Gross Receipts 1919-1938

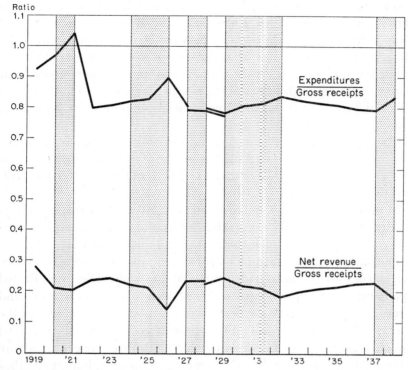

Shaded periods are contractions in ton-miles.

1917 rose to 100 per cent on August 6, 1920. Season tickets had been raised 10 per cent for journeys under 12½ miles and 20 per cent for longer journeys in May 1918; they now rose to 50 per cent above prewar. Workmen's fares, which were still at prewar, went up by varying but substantial percentages on September 1, 1920.[8]

After the postwar depression developed, the railway companies found it inexpedient to retain all of these increases. Iron ore, limestone, and certain other raw materials for blast furnaces and steel works were

[8] The changes in rates and fares are described in Railway Rates Tribunal, *Annual Report,* 1922.

Workmen's tickets were designed to provide cheap transportation to manual workers between their homes and places of employment. On the way to work they were good only on early morning trains, and their use was restricted in other respects.

(Continued on page 74)

reduced to 75 per cent above prewar on November 1, 1921, 50 per cent on May 22, 1922, and 40 per cent on December 1, 1922. Coal, coke, and patent fuel came down to 75 per cent on January 1, 1922 and 60 per cent on August 1, 1922. Special reductions were made on various other commodities. Rates on A and B commodities, not specially reduced, were lowered to 75 per cent above prewar on May 22, 1922, and those on C and Class 1 to 5 commodities were reduced to the same level on August 1, 1922. Some of the superimposed flat charges were reduced. Passenger fares other than workmen's fares and season tickets came down to 50 per cent above prewar on January 1, 1923.[4]

There were only two other general changes, and they were of less consequence. The Railway Rates Tribunal approved a general increase of 6⅔ per cent effective February 1, 1927, and another, 5 per cent, effective October 31, 1937.[5]

More piecemeal changes, intended to correct particular inequities, to attract or retain particular kinds of traffic, etc. constantly occur. The collective effect of such change over an interval of time is difficult to gauge. Data on average revenue per ton-mile and average revenue per journey are the only evidence readily available. They are affected by changes in composition of traffic as well as changes in rates and fares; in particular, revenue per journey is affected by changes in the average length of journeys. The averages are shown for peak and trough years in Table 27. Unimportant kinds of passenger traffic are omitted. Third class "ordinary" journeys are the most important; they contributed 72 per cent of all revenue from passengers, and 56 per cent of all passenger train revenue (including mail, parcels, etc.) in 1938, and the proportions were not greatly different in the other years.

Anyone who cared to travel early could buy one, however; they are now called early morning tickets.

In many cases the prewar workmen's fares were very low compared with other fares and were not systematically related to distance. Equal percentage increases were therefore not recommended. Instead, a new scale was prescribed, rising with distance and uniform for the country. No workman's fare, however, was to be increased by more than 200 per cent. See the discussion in the Rate Advisory Committee's report, reprinted in *Railway Gazette,* July 30, 1920, pp. 161 ff.

[4] *Railway Gazette,* 1922: May 19, pp. 820-1; July 14, p. 68; December 8, pp. 741-2, 767; 1923: April 27, p. 642.

[5] *Railway Returns, 1927;* Railway Rates Tribunal, *Annual Report, 1937.* All of the general increases were subject to various exceptions, maxima, minima, or other qualifications.

Ratio of Railway Expenditures to Railway Revenues and Revenue per Ton-mile and per Journey at Peaks and Troughs in Ton-miles, 1921-1938

| DATE | LEVEL OF TRAFFIC | EXPENDITURES ÷ REVENUES | REVENUE PER TON-MILE, PENCE | | | REVENUE PER PASSENGER JOURNEY, PENCE | | | |
			Merchandise	Minerals	Coal	Ordinary[a] First class	Third class	Work-men	Season tickets, third class[b]
			ABSOLUTE AMOUNTS						
1921	Trough	1.041	3.249	1.708	1.267	67.17	20.61	3.47	4.10
1924	Peak	.820	2.311	1.129	0.999	65.52	18.21	3.23	4.31
1926	Trough	.896	2.277	1.157	1.062	70.40	18.42	3.32	4.45
1927[c]	Peak	.802	2.354	1.159	1.062	69.41	17.87	3.27	4.46
1927	Peak	.793	2.401	1.155	1.057	69.39	17.87	3.27	4.46
1928[c]	Trough	.791	2.346	1.123	1.059	70.99	17.58	3.26	4.45
1928[d]	Trough	.798	2.344	1.122	1.058	74.57	18.73	3.30	4.50
1929	Peak	.781	2.267	1.103	1.043	72.42	17.43	3.36	4.50
1932	Trough	.837	2.161	1.028	1.046	64.76	15.64	3.53	4.50
1937	Peak	.794	1.948	0.966	1.037	62.81	15.83	3.55	4.44
1938	Trough	.836	2.004	0.960	1.075	66.57	17.16	3.68	4.63
			PER CENT CHANGE FROM PRECEDING DATE						
1924	Peak	−21.2	−28.9	−33.9	−21.2	−2.5	−11.6	−6.9	5.1
1926	Trough	9.3	−1.5	2.5	6.3	7.4	1.2	2.8	3.2
1927	Peak	−10.5	3.4	0.2	0.0	−1.4	−3.0	−1.5	0.2
1928	Trough	−0.3	−2.3	−2.8	0.2	2.3	−1.6	−0.3	−0.2
1929	Peak	−2.1	−3.3	−1.7	−1.4	−2.9	−6.9	1.8	0.0
1932	Trough	7.2	−4.7	−6.8	0.3	−10.6	−10.3	5.1	0.0
1937	Peak	−5.1	−9.9	−6.0	−0.9	−3.0	1.2	0.6	−1.3
1938	Trough	5.3	2.9	−0.6	3.7	6.0	8.4	3.7	4.3

[a] At full fares and at reduced fares.
[b] Average price of season tickets, adjusted to one-year basis, divided by 600.
[c] For comparison with preceding year.
[d] For comparison with following year.

After considering the history of general change in rates, and the data on revenue per ton-mile and per journey, we have formed a judgment as to the direction of change in rate level during each expansion or contraction. From the same information and the known changes in the operating ratio (Table 27), we have formed a further judgment as to the direction of change in unit cost (Table 28). In general it seems that unit cost fluctuated inversely with traffic. The exceptional rise in 1919-20 can be accounted for by the extremely rapid rise in prices of materials and supplies and in railway wage-rates. The exceptional fall in 1927-28 may be illusory and, in any case, the contraction was a very mild one. Table 28 suggests that the level of rates declined somewhat in 1929-32, but it is not clear whether the decline is enough to explain the 7.2 per cent rise in the operating ratio, or whether a rise in unit cost may also be inferred.

Effect of changes in wage rates

Unit cost is affected partly by changes in quantities of labor and materials (including fuel, etc.) used per unit of traffic and partly by changes in prices of materials and in wage-rates. Previous sections have suggested that the quantity of labor and of locomotive fuel used per unit of traffic tends to fall in expansion and rise in contraction. We have found no index of prices of railway materials, but the history of wage rates can be traced. At the beginning of 1919 they were commonly 33 shillings per week above prewar levels. In the latter part of that year and in 1920 management and unions worked out a series of agreements that standardized rates for each occupation, or "grade," at roughly twice the prewar average for each grade. The agreements provided that wages should rise and fall with the Ministry of Labour's index of the cost of living. In many grades the weekly wage was to change one shilling for each 5-point change in the index. Declines in the cost of living, however, were not to reduce the rate paid below the standard rate. These provisions brought further increases in rates during 1920 and reductions during 1921 and 1922.[6] Thereafter the cost of living occasionally raised or lowered rates a shilling or two per week, or brought standard rates into effect, but on the whole there

[6] On the changes in wage rates and arrangements see the *Railway Gazette* for 1920, especially January 9, pp. 44-6; January 23, pp. 115-6; February 20, p. 266; February 27, p. 301; May 2, p. 514; June 11, p. 858; October 8, p. 475; December 13, p. 727; also December 28, 1923, pp. 831-2.

TABLE 28

Direction of Change in Operating Ratio, Rate Level, and Unit Cost
during Traffic Expansions and Contractions, 1919-1938

		DIRECTION OF CHANGE	
	Operating	Rate	Unit
Expansions	ratio	level	cost
1919-20	+	+	+
1921-24	−	−	−
1926-27	−	+	−
1928-29	−	little change	−
1932-37	−	−?	−
Contractions			
1920-21	+	+	+
1924-26	+	little change	+
1927-28	−	little change	−
1929-32	+	−?	little change?
1937-38	+	+	+

For derivation, see text.

was little change in the going rates.[7] During most of the ten years
beginning August 1928, however, it was agreed that, after each wage
payment had been computed in accordance with the going rates and
rules, a percentage should be deducted from the sum so obtained. But
the percentages were small, and the changes in them did not correspond closely in time with traffic or business cycles (Table 29). We
conclude that changes in wage-rates tended strongly to raise unit cost
in the 1919-20 and to reduce it in the 1921-24 expansion, but that in
other expansions and contractions they had little effect on unit cost.

Return on investment varied directly with traffic

With one possible exception, in 1929-32, the direction of change was
the same in the operating ratio as in unit cost (Table 28). Rises and
falls in unit cost, therefore, were not accompanied by proportional rises
or falls in the average charge for railway services. The latter were
inflexible enough to cause changes in unit cost to be reflected in opposite changes in the ratio of railway net receipts to revenue.

Even if net receipts were a constant proportion of gross, aggregate

[7] We base this remark on detailed study of the grade-by-grade data on "rate of
wages payable" or "average weekly salary or wage" in the various issues of *Railway
Returns — Staff*.

net receipts would rise in expansion and fall in contraction, for aggregate gross receipts usually rose and fell with traffic. Since the aggregate net receipts fluctuate more than the gross, their rise and fall is more pronounced. Net receipts are not the same thing as net revenue, to which railway security holders must look for a return on their investment. To arrive at net revenue, one must add to net railway receipts

TABLE **29**

Percentage Deductions from Earnings of Railway Employees, 1928-1937

DATE FIRST EFFECTIVE	CONCILIATION GRADES[a] Per cent	Extra Per cent[b]	MECHANICS AND ARTISANS Per cent
August 13, 1928	2½	0	2½
May 13, 1930	n o	d e d u c t i o n	
March 28, 1931[c]	2½	2½	4⅙[d]
October 1, 1934[c]	2½	1¼	3⅓
January 1, 1935[c]	2½	0	2½
August 26, 1936[c,e]	1¼	0	1¼
August 16, 1937[c,e]	n o	d e d u c t i o n	

[a] In 1907 a system of boards for the conciliation of disputes between railway companies and their employees was established. Occupations embraced in these arrangements came to be known as Conciliation Grades. The term includes most railway employees other than mechanics and artisans.
[b] On excess of earnings over 40s. per week (wage earners) or £100 per year (salaried workers).
[c] Effective in first full pay period after this date, except conciliation grades in 1937.
[d] i.e. 10 pence in the pound.
[e] Mechanics and artisans, July 1.
Compiled from information in *Railway Gazette*, August 3, 1928, p. 134; March 13, 1931, p. 422; March 20, 1931, pp. 465, 502; August 17, 1934, p. 284; October 5, 1934, p. 559; July 3, 1936, p. 17; August 7, 1936, pp. 220, 222; August 13, 1937, pp. 297-8. See also *Railway Returns, Staff*, 1931, 1938.

the net receipts from the various but less important other enterprises of the railway companies (e.g. steamboats, hotels) and certain miscellaneous kinds of income, and one must deduct certain miscellaneous charges. But railway net receipts are by far the largest element in net revenue, and the ratio of net revenue to railway gross receipts has usually varied inversely with traffic, like the ratio of railway net receipts to gross. (Chart 25. The ratio of railway net receipts to gross is measured by the vertical interval between the expense ratio and unity.) A salient exception in 1920-21 will be explained in a moment.

The investment in the railways, on the other hand, was more stable than their revenue, and the companies earned a higher rate of return

CHART 26

Return on Total Assets and on Net Worth, 1920-1938

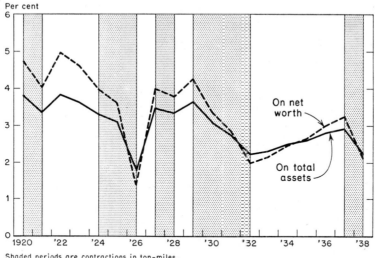

Per cent

On net worth

On total assets

Shaded periods are contractions in ton-miles.

on their transportation property and other investments in times of good business and heavy traffic (Chart 26).[8] From 1920 onward, peaks and troughs in the ratio of net revenue to total assets coincided with those in the reference chronology and in net ton-miles, except in the 1921-24 expansion, when earnings reached a peak very early. The net decline in this phase, however, is smaller than in the next contraction. Fluctuations in the rate of return on net worth coincided in time with those in return on total assets, but were greater in amplitude, since interest charges on funded debt varied little from year to year.

[8] The customary statistical balance sheet for British railways did not include among the assets the entire quasi-permanent investment; instead it showed the excess of "capital expenditure" over "capital receipts" from bonds, debentures and stocks, none of which appeared as a liability. In our computations, total assets = capital receipts + capital expenditures in excess of capital receipts + other balance sheet assets. Net worth = total assets − bonds and debentures ("amount on which interest is payable") − balance sheet liabilities except "balance available for dividends and general reserve. . . ." Year-end figures thus computed are averaged to derive the base on which the return for each year is computed. Return on total assets = net revenue ÷ average assets for year × 100. Return on net worth = (net revenue − interest on bonds and debentures) ÷ average net worth × 100.

All figures used include through 1932 the railways taken over by the London Passenger Transport Board, exclude them thereafter. Computations for 1928-32, leaving them out, indicate that the effect of inclusion or exclusion on the rate of return is very slight.

Because of financial arrangements with the government, the net revenue of the railway companies does not reflect the low level of operating profits in 1920 or the deficit in 1921 (Table 30). If we

TABLE **30**

Income Account of Railways, 1920-1922

		1920	1921	1922
		(thousands of pounds)		
(1)	Gross receipts from operations	257,974[a]	236,312	238,224
(2)	Operating expenditure	252,036	246,156	191,075
(3)	Net receipts, (1) − (2)	5,938	−9,844	47,149
(4)	Government compensation[b]	41,030[c]	51,339	......
(5)	Miscellaneous receipts[d]	4,392	4,515	6,216
(6)	Miscellaneous charges[d]	1,943	2,005	2,019
(7)	Net revenue, (3) + (4) + (5) − (6)[e]	49,417	44,005	51,346
(8)	Net revenue before government compensation, (7) − (4)	8,387	−7,334	51,346

[a] Includes £1,492 thousand, estimated value of services rendered to government without specific charge.
[b] Continuing under wartime arrangements in 1920, the railroads operated for the account of the government, which paid them their prewar earnings as rent for the use of their properties. In 1921 they operated for their own account but with a transitional guarantee of earnings.
[c] Compensation in excess of estimated value of services, note a.
[d] Net rents, miscellaneous interest, etc.
[e] Does not appear in official financial statement before 1927, but computable as indicated.

deduct government compensation from net revenue, the remainder — line (8) — is equivalent to 0.65 per cent of total assets in 1920 and to a negative return, −0.56 per cent, in 1921. Deducting government compensation from net revenue minus interest on funded debt yields a negative return on net worth in both years, −.44 per cent in the first, and −2.42 per cent in the second.

7. Traffic and Operations since 1938

Business, war, and traffic

The authors of the business chronology employed in this paper did not carry it beyond 1938. The war affected diverse economic activities in diverse ways after that year (Table 31). Some promptly fell below, and remained below, their 1938 level. Others revived, but in important cases the rise came to an end quite early and was followed by a decline. Toward the end of the war declines were rather general. Perhaps if all the relevant evidence were assembled and considered it would point to a trough in general business activity somewhere in 1945.

Railway freight traffic revived promptly and continued to grow (except for a slight relapse in 1940-41) to a peak in 1943 (if we consider tonnage) or 1944 (if we consider ton-miles) (Table 32). Quarterly data on ton-miles, which became available in 1944, suggest a peak in the third quarter of that year. Most of the increase occurred in 1938-39.

Passenger traffic rose from its belated trough in 1940 to a peak in 1945. Journeys of the armed forces and other travel on government business accounted for a large part but by no means all of the rise (Table 33).

The subsequent contractions of freight and passenger traffic can be traced in more detail from quarterly or monthly data (Charts 27, 28). The movement of goods, after attaining a peak in the third quarter of 1944, declined to a trough in the first quarter of 1947.[1]

[1] Heavy shipments of goods to the Channel in support of the invasion and later of the armies in France account for the location of this peak. The number of special freight trains run for the government per quarter had increased gradually to 14,307 in the first quarter of 1944; it rose to 24,816 in the second and 32,226 in the third, after which it declined. R. Bell, *History of the British Railways during the War, 1939-45* (London, published by Railway Gazette, 1946), p. 267.

In the first quarter of 1947 Britain suffered almost unprecedented heavy snows.

(Continued on page 82)

TABLE 31

Economic Activity in Great Britain, 1938-1946

KIND OF ACTIVITY	UNIT OF MEASURE-MENT	IN 1938 Amount	IN HIGHEST WAR YEAR[a] Date	IN HIGHEST WAR YEAR[a] Amount	IN LOWEST YEAR Date	IN LOWEST YEAR Amount
Houses built[b]	Thousands	332.4	......	......	1944	5.5
Cotton disposals	Thous. tons	515	......	......	1945	338
Raw wool consumption	Thous. tons	c	c	c	1944	115
Imports, at 1938 prices	1938 = 100	100.0	......	......	1945	61.9
Exports, at 1938 prices	1938 = 100	100.0	......	......	1943	29.0
Coal production	Mill. tons	227	1939	231	1945	183
Steel ingot production[d]	Mill. tons	10.4	1939	13.2	1945	11.8
Ships built	Thous. tons	1030	1942	1302	1945	743
Electricity generated	Bill. k.w.h.	25.7	1944	39.6	1945	38.6
Workers in civil employment	Millions	17.4	1939	18.0	1945	16.4

[a] Shown only for activities that exceeded their 1938 level in some war year.
[b] Including flats, each flat being counted as one unit. Years beginning April 1. England and Wales only.
[c] 1938-39 not available. Declined continuously from 239 thousand tons in 1940 to 1944.
[d] Includes castings.
Compiled from *Annual Abstract of Statistics*.

After a fall in the first half of 1944 and a rise in the second half, passenger traffic declined from March 1945 to an apparent trough in August 1948.[2] This long decline during a period of business expansion is explained partly by the cessation of military movements and the gradually slackening pace of demobilization and partly by the resumption of private motoring. The number of persons in the Armed Forces and Auxiliary Services in June diminished by 3,058 thousand in 1945-46, 730 thousand in 1946-47, and 456 thousand in 1947-48. Motor fuel was severely rationed during the war; many car owners put their vehicles in storage and allowed the licenses to lapse. After the first quarter of 1945 licenses were rapidly renewed, indicating a great increase in use of cars, part of it no doubt for journeys that would

They and a coal shortage interfered with railway operations to some extent (*Railway Gazette,* February 7, p. 175; March 7, pp. 200, 213). But the general trend of traffic was downward in earlier and upward in later quarters. Even if the weather had been normal there would have been a trough somewhere in this neighborhood.

[2] Although February 1944 was higher than March 1945 we do not take it as a peak because we do not know what happened two months before, and because the annual data suggest a steady rise to 1945.

TABLE **32**

Freight Traffic and Operating Statistics, 1937-1947

	TONS ORIGI- NATED[a] (mil- lions)	NET TON- MILES[b] (bil- lions)	NET TON- MILES PER LOADED WAGON MILE	LOADED WAGON MILES PER TRAIN MILE	NET TON- MILES PER TRAIN MILE	TRAIN MILES PER TRAIN HOUR	NET TON- MILES PER TRAIN HOUR
1937[c]	297[d]	18.38	5.65	23.20	131.1	8.61	1,129
1938[e]	264[d]	16.67	5.55	22.49	124.9	9.15	1,142
1938[e]	266	16.27	5.42	22.49	121.8	9.15	1,114
1939	288	f	f	f	f	8.70	f
1940	294	f	f	f	f	7.33	f
1941	287	f	f	25.41	f	7.16	f
1942	295	23.82	5.98	25.63	152.8	7.23	1,105
1943	301	24.36	6.01	26.00	156.0	7.32	1,142
1944	293	24.44	6.01	26.21	157.7	7.14	1,126
1945	266	22.02	5.98	25.92	154.5	7.44	1,149
1946	262	20.64	5.99	25.33	151.2	7.64	1,155
1947	257	20.19	6.23	24.78	153.8	7.58	1,276

[a] Excluding free-hauled.
[b] Including free-hauled.
[c] Basic data from *Railway Returns*.
[d] Excluding livestock.
[e] Basic data, like those for later years, from *Annual Abstract of Statistics*. Lower 1938 ratios derived from this source result from the smaller figure it gives for aggregate ton-miles.
[f] Not available.

otherwise have been taken by rail. Apparently new petrol troubles caused a temporary drop in licenses during the winter of 1947-48; the rail traffic shows a corresponding rise.[3]

Operations during the war cycle

The increase in ton-miles from 1938 to 1944 was accompanied, as usual, by a rise in the average carload, the number of loaded cars in a

[3] The number of journeys rose abruptly in September 1947 and fell abruptly in October. The disturbance was confined to the season ticket business. Prices of these tickets were raised from 25 per cent above prewar to 55 per cent, effective October 1. Users rushed to buy them before the price went up. Fares for single journeys also rose, but habitual users who purchase many journeys by means of a single document can act in anticipation of a rise more conveniently than occasional travelers.

TABLE **33**
Passenger Traffic and Operating Statistics, 1937-1946

	NUMBER OF JOURNEYS			TRAIN MILES
	Service and			PER
	government, etc.	*Total*	TRAIN MILES	TRAIN HOUR
	(*millions*)			
1937	a	1,295	283.4	14.97
1938	53.6	1,237	287.4	15.08
1939	53.4	1,226	256.9	14.76
1940	77.7	967	201.3	13.23
1941	116.1	1,023	201.9	13.16
1942	163.7	1,218	203.2	13.38
1943	227.4	1,335	204.2	13.54
1944	250.5	1,345	202.1	13.48
1945	256.9	1,372	215.8	13.86
1946	147.5	1,266	236.9	14.32

a Not available.

train and the average trainload (Table 32). But, again as usual, the speed of trains declined, and there was little improvement in the amount of traffic movement during a train hour. On the other hand, the 42 per cent increase in the number of passengers from 1940 to 1945 was cared for by an increase of only 14.5 million train-miles, or 7 per cent (Table 33). The number of passengers in a train obviously increased and, since the average speed rose a little, the amount of passenger movement performed per train hour also increased.[4]

During the 1944-47 contraction in ton-miles, the average wagonload did not decline but the gain during the preceding expansion was halted (Chart 27). The number of loaded wagon-miles, and the tonmiles, per train-mile did decline. But, once more, speed increased and hourly train performance rose from 1,126 ton-miles in 1944 to 1,276 in 1947.[5] Coaching train-miles increased during the 1945-48 contrac-

[4] The 1937-40 contraction in travel was unusual in that coaching train miles were curtailed 29 per cent, a drop greater than the decline in the number of passengers, 25 per cent. At first to minimize exposure to air raids, and later to make way for urgently needed freight, many of the passenger trains in the prewar timetable were eliminated. The scheduled time of many others was lengthened. See Bell, Chapter 10 and p. 266. The sharp 1938-40 cut, and the restriction of increase thereafter, were accomplished at a cost in terms of discomfort and inconvenience to passengers that would be tolerated only in a wartime economy. From 1937 to 1938, on the other hand, train-miles actually increased in spite of the decline in travel.

[5] 1947 was the trough *year* in ton-miles. There are no quarterly data on speeds, and hence none on hourly performance, for 1944-46.

CHART 27

Freight Traffic and Operations
First Quarter 1944-Fourth Quarter 1952

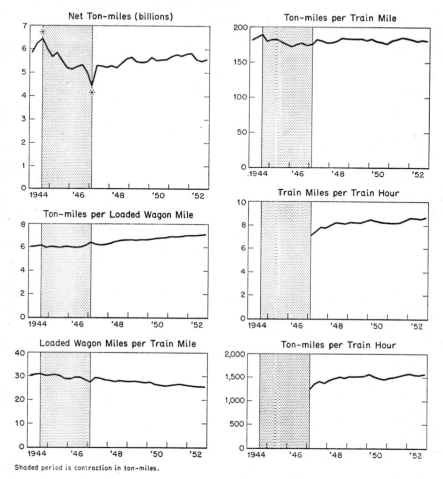

Shaded period is contraction in ton-miles.

tion in travel (Chart 28); in part at least, however, this development reflects an effort to get back to prewar standards of frequency and convenience.[6]

Stocks of equipment altered little during the war and early postwar years. The railroads were able to handle their 50 per cent increase in

[6] This was certainly true in 1948. See British Transport Commission, *Report and Accounts* for 1948, p. 78.

TABLE 34
Changes in Equipment and in Traffic during War Cycle

	AT INITIAL TROUGH	AT PEAK	AT TERMI- NAL TROUGH	PER CENT CHANGE Expan- sion	Con- traction
Freight service					
Year	1938	1944	1947	1938-44	1944-47
Net ton-miles (billions)	16.27	24.44	20.19	50.2	−17.4
Trucks and wagons (thousands)[a]					
Railway owned, operating stock	660	685	660	3.8	−3.6
Railway owned, available[b]	641	646	586	0.8	−9.3
Privately owned, operating stock	[c]	610	594	....	−2.6
Privately owned, available[b,d]	[c]	550	497	....	−9.6
Passenger service					
Year	1940	1945	1948[e]	1940-45	1945-48
Number of journeys (millions)	967	1,372	996	41.9	−27.4
Passenger-carrying vehicles (thousands)[a,f]					
Operating stock	42.7	40.5	40.4	−5.2	−0.2
Available[b]	40.1	36.3	35.8	−9.5	−1.4

[a] Average of figures for end of year and end of preceding year.
[b] Excluding vehicles under or awaiting repair.
[c] No data. 638 thousand owned in July 1937 and 605 thousand at end of 1939.
[d] Does not include vehicles not requisitioned for railway operation. There were few of these.
[e] The annual number of journeys was slightly smaller in 1949 and 1950 than in 1948; but monthly data suggest a trough in 1948. Cf. Chart 28.
[f] Includes rail motor cars.

freight traffic with only a 4 per cent increase in the number of wagons (Table 34). Indeed some wagons were allowed to fall into and remain in disrepair, for the serviceable stock increased only one per cent. The 42 per cent rise in passenger traffic was actually accompanied by a decline in the total stock of passenger-carrying vehicles and a greater decline in the usable stock. Conversely the declines in traffic at the end of the war were greater than the declines in stocks of wagons and carriages. The number of locomotives cannot be subdivided by branch of service, but the highest figure for "operating stock," in all services, in the period 1938-48 (20,611 locomotives, at the end of 1943), is only 5.9 per cent larger than the lowest figure (19,461 at the end of 1941). The highest figure for "available" stock (16,812, at the end

CHART 28

**Rail Journeys, and Related Data
January 1944-December 1952**

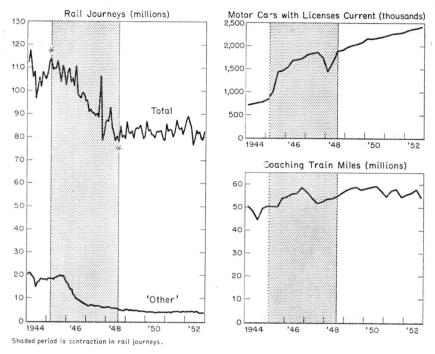

Rail Journeys (millions)

Motor Cars with Licenses Current (thousands)

Coaching Train Miles (millions)

Shaded period is contraction in rail journeys.

of 1943) is 5.1 per cent above the lowest figure (15,991, at the end of 1946). As usual, the railroads were able to deal with heavier traffic by keeping their equipment in use more of the time. The changes in loads, hourly performance, and use of equipment during the war cycles in freight and passenger traffic were broadly similar to those we found in peacetime cycles.

The financial results, too, resembled in some respects those encountered in times of peace. An increase in operating revenues from 1940 to 1944 was accompanied by a falling operating ratio except in the last year (Table 35. Comparable data for 1938 and 1939 are not available). As revenue declined after 1944, the operating ratio rose until expenses exceeded revenues in 1947.

The rise in the margin of profit from 1940 to 1943 must be attributed to the growth of traffic, for changes in price relations were unfavorable to profits. Except for moderate increases in 1940, rates and

87

TABLE 35
Operating Revenues, Expenses, and Profits, 1940-51

	GROSS OPERATING RECEIPTS (1)	OPERATING EXPENDITURE (2)	NET OPERATING RECEIPTS, (1) − (2) (3)	OPERATING RATIO, (2) ÷ (1) × 100 (4)
		Millions of pounds		
1940	248.0	203.5	44.5	82.1
1941	293.8	226.6	67.2	77.1
1942	343.5	251.7	91.8	73.3
1943	381.7	272.2	109.5	71.3
1944	394.4	301.2	93.2	76.4
1945	383.9	317.0	66.9	82.6
1946	360.7	325.2	35.5	90.2
1947	355.6	367.2	−11.6	103.3
1948	336.1	309.9	26.2	92.2
1949	325.5	312.8	12.7	96.1
1950	340.1	313.7	26.4	92.2
1951	372.7	337.8	34.9	90.6

1940-47, four main railways and London Passenger Transport Board. 1948-51, Railway Executive; operations of London Transport Executive not included.

fares were stable (Table 36). The Board of Trade price indexes most appropriate to a discussion of railway purchases suggest that prices of railway materials and supplies increased. Workers on the railways received successive increases in wages and salaries.[7]

The adverse effect of declining traffic on profits was probably reenforced during 1944-47 by further unfavorable realignments of prices received and paid. Prices of materials and supplies apparently rose faster than rates and fares. Wage rates were advanced in 1945 and again in 1947, but their average percentage rise over the full 1944-47 period cannot be computed and we do not know whether it exceeded the percentage rise in the changes for railway services.

The high operating profits during the war years did not benefit railway stockholders. Beginning in 1940, railway earnings, including those of the LPTB, were pooled. The government guaranteed to the railways an annual net revenue based on prewar figures, and retained the excess, if any. The arrangement continued through 1947; on January

[7] See *Ministry of Labour Gazette*, Feb., March, July, 1940; May, June, 1941; April, Sept., Oct., 1942; Jan., July, 1943; May, 1944.

TABLE 36
Indexes of Prices of Railway Services and of Wholesale Prices

| | RAILWAY SERVICES | | | WHOLESALE PRICES[a] | |
	Freight rates	*Passenger fares*	*Coal*	*Iron and steel*	*Nonferrous metals*
	1937[b] = 100			1938 = 100	
1940	109[c,d]	109[c,d]	113.7	114.5	130.5
1941	117	117	129.5	130.2	131.3
1942	117	117	138.9	131.2	133.3
1943	117	117	150.8	131.4	133.5
1944	117	117	169.7	132.4	135.4
1945	117	117	192.4	135.7	134.6
1946	121[c,e]	125[c,e]	198.1	150.4	159.8
1947	132[c,f]	139[c,f]	204.4	159.2	235.6
			1940 = 100[g]		
1940	100	100	100	100	100
1941	107	107	114	114	101
1942	107	107	122	115	102
1943	107	107	133	115	102
1944	107	107	149	116	104
			1944 = 100[g]		
1944	100	100	100	100	100
1945	100	100	113	102	99
1946	103	107	117	114	118
1947	113	119	120	120	174

[a] Board of Trade indexes.
[b] Prior to October 1.
[c] Average weighted by number of months rates were in effect.
[d] Rates and fares were increased 5 per cent on October 1, 1937: increase became 10 per cent on May 1, 1940 and 16⅔ per cent on December 1, 1940.
[e] On July 1, 1946 increase over 1937 became 25 per cent for rates and 33⅓ per cent for fares.
[f] On October 1, 1947 increase over 1937 became 55 per cent.
[g] Figure above for each year divided by corresponding figure for 1940 or 1944.

1, 1948 the railways became public property. Although the government suffered a heavy loss in 1947 it made a handsome profit over the entire period 1940-47.

The postwar expansion

The data in Table 31 suggest that the British economy was expanding from 1945 to 1946. A new monthly index of industrial production, prepared by the Central Statistical Office, indicates that the expansion continued thereafter. Converting the "interim" index for 1946 and 1947 to a 1948 base, linking it with a revised index for later periods, and seasonally adjusting the figures, we find that industrial production increased from 74 per cent of 1948 in January 1946 to 123 per cent in April 1951; since then it has declined a little. The growth of output was not only prolonged but steady, except for a temporary set-back caused by the extreme winter weather early in 1947. (Seasonal adjustment of data does not "eliminate" the effects of *extraordinarily* bad weather.)

Rising production was not reflected in rail traffic until after the 1947 disturbance (Chart 27). Ton-miles increased from the first quarter of that year to the first quarter of 1952; more recently they appear to have diminished.

The average wagon-load improved much more distinctly during this expansion of traffic than in earlier expansions. Special influences as well as the usual cyclical processes were at work. One of these was a change in the character of equipment. When the British socialized their coal industry, the new National Coal Board inherited the private rail wagons that formerly belonged to the mine owners. When rail transport was nationalized in 1948, the Coal Board turned these vehicles over to the British Transport Commission, which operates the railroads through its subsidiary, the Railway Executive. Many of the formerly private wagons were antiquated, and the Executive began to break them up. Of 544 thousand acquired, 55,000 were demolished in 1948; 68,000 were withdrawn from service in 1949; 31,000 in 1950; and 27,000 in 1951. They were comparatively small. At the 1937 census, privately owned coal wagons could carry, on the average, only 10.91 tons; wagons owned by railways at the end of the year could carry 11.93 tons. While the Executive was getting rid of this equipment it was also acquiring new vehicles of more than average size. Between the end of 1948 and the end of 1951 the average capacity of all its wagons, old and new, increased from 12.50 to 13.16 tons, at a rate of 0.22 tons per year. The increase for railway-owned wagons from the end of 1921 to the end of 1938 was only 0.10 tons per annum.

In view of the pronounced change in the average load, it is perhaps not surprising that in this expansion of traffic the number of loaded cars per train diminished, although it increased in previous expansions. But one would still expect the growth of traffic to be accompanied by an increase in the average amount of freight in a train; actually, however, there was little change in net ton-miles per train-mile.

During the interwar expansions growth of traffic had reduced the speed of freight trains. In the present instance, however, the Executive took special steps of a permanent character to expedite movement, and the average speed increased in 1947-1951. Hourly performance — ton-miles per train hour — consequently improved, even though there was no improvement in ton-miles per train *mile*.

Except for minor and temporary fluctuations, the number of people riding in trains has been remarkably constant since early 1948 (Chart 28). The growing attraction of motor travel almost exactly offset the normal stimulating effect of business expansion on rail travel.

The Executive did not, on balance, reduce the amount of service offered, measured in train miles. This business expansion was not accompanied by the usual, cost-reducing rise in passenger train loads.

Although freight traffic increased, and passenger traffic diminished very little, the revenues of the Railway Executive declined from 1948 to 1949 (Table 35). Higher charges contributed to the subsequent revival. Freight rates were raised 16⅔ per cent on May 15, 1950; and the rates thus established were raised 10 per cent on April 16, 1951. From year to year the operating ratio varied inversely with revenue. A final profit figure after deductions other than operating expenses is not computed for the railways separately. A "balance on net revenue account" is reported for all BTC undertakings combined — railways, London Transport, road and water transport, hotels, etc. The balance for the first year was a deficit, £4.7 million, which deepened to £20.8 million as operating revenue fell. As the latter revived, the deficit was reduced to £14.1 in 1950 and was succeeded by a very small positive balance, £0.1 million, in 1951.[8]

---

[8] BTC's accounting system differs considerably from the system that prevailed under private ownership. Depreciation charges on much of the property are now computed and included in operating expense. For this reason among others, operating ratios before nationalization are not closely comparable with operating ratios afterward. The concept of "balance on net revenue account" differs widely from the old "net revenue." Deductions made in computing the "balance" include not only write-offs and other items but amortization of the British Transport Stock (government debt) issued in exchange for railways and other properties.

8. Britain and the United States

British transport differs in many ways from American transport. For example, passenger traffic is more important, relative to freight traffic, in Britain than in the United States. Hauls and journeys are much shorter there. British cars, carloads, and trainloads are smaller. The amount of labor required on the railroads is larger in proportion to traffic. But the cyclical experience of British transport enterprises has been broadly similar to that of American enterprises. The following generalizations apply to both countries, except when we draw a specific contrast between them.[1]

Traffic

Fluctuations in traffic correspond in a general way to disturbances in economic activity at large. Before World War I, business contractions were sometimes accompanied by retardations in the growth of rail traffic (if we may trust the annual data), rather than by actual declines. Even when traffic diminished, the next expansion of business usually raised it to higher levels than were ever attained before. After the war, on the contrary, there was little net growth from one peak to the next, or one trough to the next; indeed, in some cycles there was a net decline, especially in passenger traffic. The growing attractiveness of motor transport helps to explain the change in the rail trend. (The rate of growth in motor vehicle registrations and in gasoline consumption was maintained more vigorously after 1929 in Britain than in the United States.) The railroads lost traffic to their new competitors more rapidly in contractions of business than in expansions (British data are less adequate on this point).

[1] The discussion is based on the conclusions about Britain in the preceding sections of this paper, and those about the United States in my monograph, *American Transportation in Prosperity and Depression* (National Bureau of Economic Research, 1948).

The tonnage of durable goods that the railways carry fluctuates more than their tonnage of nondurables. Since railways haul the products and raw materials of many industries, their traffic and earnings are affected both by the mild cyclical disturbances in some parts of the economy and by the severe shocks in other parts. Fluctuations in aggregate freight traffic cannot be ranked among the mildest or among the most extreme of disturbances. Passenger travel by rail is more stable than freight traffic. Season ticket holders in Britain, like commuters in the United States, vary their patronage of the railways remarkably little during the course of a business cycle. Fluctuations in travel by street car and bus, or by private motor car, are also mild.

Are cyclical disturbances in business at large less severe in Britain than in the United States? Many economic activities should be examined for an answer, but data on rail traffic might be helpful. The annual figures for both countries before World War I, however, disclose few contractions in freight and even fewer in passenger traffic. In most of these the decline in tons or passengers carried was 5 per cent or less. The severity of the earlier postwar British fluctuations was accentuated by the great strikes; events like these, fortunately, are not typical of depressions. From 1927, or at least from 1929, to 1938, fluctuations in American freight traffic, both upwards and downwards, were decidedly more severe, percentagewise, than those in British freight traffic (Table 37). Rail passenger travel in Britain had no expansion comparable in time with the 1928-29 expansion in the United States, and no contraction comparable with 1937-38. But the 1929-33 fall in American rail travel, and the subsequent rise ending in 1937, were much greater than their British analogues.

Operations and maintenance

When rail freight traffic expands, the average size of the loads in freight cars is likely to increase, and so is the number of loaded cars in a train; trainloads become heavier.[2] Although loads improve, lines become more congested; trains are slowed, and make more frequent and lengthier halts. The decline in train-miles per train hour is sometimes large enough to offset the rise in ton-miles per train-mile; in such instances, an hour of train operation accomplishes no more movement

[2] In part at least, the average load is high near a peak in traffic because commodities that are always heavily loaded comprise a larger percentage of all traffic in prosperity.

TABLE 37
Comparative Severity of Rail Traffic Cycles, 1927-1938

| Level of traffic | GREAT BRITAIN | | | UNITED STATES | | |
	Date level reached	Amount[a]	% Change from preceding date	Date level reached	Amount[a]	% Change from preceding date
			TON-MILES[b]			
Trough	July 1928	1,476	......	Dec. 1927	34.13	......
Peak	Nov. 1929	1,595	8	Aug. 1929	37.84	11
Trough	Dec. 1932	1,198	—25	July 1932	17.11	—55
Peak	June 1937	1,575	31	Apr. 1937	33.06	93
Trough	Aug. 1938	1,339	—15	May 1938	22.88	—31
			NUMBER OF PASSENGERS[c]			
Peak	May 1929	71.6	......	Mar. 1929	27.9	......
Trough	Apr. 1932	64.0	—11	Mar. 1933	11.6	—58
Peak	May 1937	77.8	22	Mar. 1937	21.5	85

[a] Billions of ton-miles; millions of passengers. Average for month indicated, preceding, and following month.
[b] Revenue and non-revenue ton-miles, G.B.; revenue, U.S.
[c] Since monthly British data including journeys of season-ticket holders are not available, we use number of U.S. passengers excluding commuters. U.S. figures are from unpublished worksheets based on ICC data.

of goods than before. In the United States, however, technological progress increased the average speed even during some of the traffic expansions, although not as rapidly as in the contractions. In America, therefore, congestion did not neutralize the favorable effect of higher loads on hourly performance to the same extent as in Britain.

The rise in loads tends to reduce train labor expense, in spite of the drop in speed. The rules governing wage payment differ from one country to the other, but in both the lengthening of the time required to complete a run does not increase the wages of the crew unless it is great enough to bring the overtime provisions into play.

In passenger service, the number of travelers in a train increases during an expansion of aggregate rail travel. Speed is not affected much, as these trains are given priority. There is an improvement in hourly performance. Wages of train crews and other expenses connected with the running of passenger trains tend to decline relatively to the amount of travel.

Managers of railways do not increase their stocks of equipment in proportion to traffic during an expansion of the latter. They deal with the growth of tonnage or of travel largely by more intensive use of rolling stock.

All these effects are reversed in contractions of traffic. Trainloads diminish, train expenses per ton-mile or per passenger-mile tend to rise, the initial stock of equipment mostly remains on hand or even increases and vehicles are less intensively used.

What is true of train labor is true of railway labor in the aggregate. The number of hours that must be paid for rises less than traffic, and it tends to fall less than traffic, although technological progress sometimes keeps the tendency from working out. In the United States at least, manhours actually worked fluctuate less than traffic. (There are no data for Britain.)

Locomotives in freight service do not increase or decrease their consumption of fuel in proportion to the rise or fall in ton-miles. Fuel consumed in passenger service does not fluctuate as much, percentagewise, as passenger-miles, in the United States, and probably not in Britain. (Again, no data.)

We investigated different aspects of maintenance work in the two countries. In the United States we found that manhours paid for in this kind of work are, if anything, somewhat more stable than traffic. In Britain, repairs to equipment are about as stable as traffic, on an average, while the quantities of materials used in maintenance of way are somewhat more stable.

Costs and financial returns

Prices of commodities used in railway operations rise during a business expansion and fall during a contraction, in the United States and very likely in Britain also (where, however, we have found no approximation to an index of such prices). In both, changes in wage-rates are related very loosely to cycles in traffic or business. On the other hand, labor requirements, fuel requirements, and probably requirements of some materials, fall, on a per-unit-of-traffic basis, in expansion and rise in contraction.[3] The change in prices tends to raise and lower cost per traffic unit in positive conformity to the course of a cycle, while the

[3] In what follows, we assume that traffic and business change in the same direction most of the time. This was true in the interwar period, to which most of our operating and financial data pertain.

change in unit requirements tends to make unit cost vary inversely with traffic and business. During most of the interwar cycles the changes in requirements were more potent than the changes in prices paid, for unit cost usually fell in expansions and rose in contractions. (This is clearer in the U. S. than in Britain.)

The prices the railways charge for their services are usually more stable than their unit costs. Hence the ratio of costs to revenue falls in expansions and rises in contractions. Profit margins rise and fall with traffic, and so, of course, do aggregate profits. The accumulated investment in railways changes only gradually, and the rate of return on investment rises and falls with traffic.

9.   Toward Understanding Cycles

The original purpose of the investigation described in this paper was largely descriptive. General disturbances in economic activity can hardly be understood until they have been identified in time and space with some particularity. During what periods, in each of the major industrial countries, was the growth of business enterprise interrupted? Were some of the interruptions brief and mild, while others were severe and protracted? What of the intervening expansions? For answers to such questions, many economic activities should be examined. The activities of transport enterprises and their customers must rank high on any list. Railways have played a central part in modern economic development. They carry almost everything that industry produces, and their freight traffic is therefore a broad if rough measure of industrial production. Railway statistics for Britain before World War I are especially valuable because direct measures of industrial production in that period are very limited.

The railway data confirm, in an approximate manner, the Burns-Mitchell chronology. Cycles in railway traffic correspond in a general way with the cycles that, according to the chronology, occurred in business at large. Even when traffic did not decline in the business contractions, its rate of growth was retarded.

Some investigators of business cycles have been fascinated by the thought that they were dealing with a phenomenon of regularly recurring frequency and magnitude. A glance at the railway traffic data in Table 6 should leave any reader skeptical of simple periodic theories. Either there is no tendency toward periodicity, or the effects of that tendency are deeply buried among the effects of non-periodic influences, or several different periodicities are concurrently and complexly interwoven.

The various aspects of economic life differ greatly in degree of disturbance. Passenger traffic is less variable than freight traffic; the latter is more stable than production of steel. Changes in the composition of freight traffic provide additional evidence that fluctuations in durable goods industries are more severe than those in other industries.

We have described the operations of British railways in fairly intensive detail from 1919 to 1952. In 9 of these 34 years they and the British economy at large were directly affected by war or by great strikes with very general consequences. To what extent should we draw distinctions between the cycles in which these events figured and other cycles? The railway operating concomitants of the traffic changes in the 1921 and 1926 strikes were different from the operating concomitants of other fluctuations in traffic. The 1926 strike may have dislocated the sequence of prosperity and depression for several years; the annual reference chronology for Britain is curiously out of step with the chronology for the United States from 1925 to 1928. Here is meat for those who like problems of definition.

Notation of features like those briefly mentioned in the preceding paragraphs is part of the descriptive task. Lively minds will not be content with descriptions, but will wish to know why general economic disturbances occur, and why some are more violent or prolonged than others. Strikes and wars explain some characteristics of some disturbances, but they do not obviously explain a cycle like 1879-86 or 1932-38. Transportation data alone will hardly provide explanations. But they nevertheless have some relevance to various lines of thought along which the problem has been approached.

In recent years there has been much discussion of the stimulating effects that are supposed to flow from an increase in expenditures on plant, equipment, and inventories. Under favorable circumstances, the increase of investment is believed to induce a much larger increase of expenditure on goods for consumption. There is a "multiplier" effect on employment and presumably on the volume of traffic offered for transportation. On the other hand, one can readily imagine circumstances under which the increment of investment will express itself primarily in an inflation of prices. In weighing such possibilities it seems pertinent to note that an increase in railway traffic will ordinarily be accompanied by a less than proportionate increase in railway employment and purchases, and that the situation in some other industries is probably similar. Conversely, influences depressing traffic will have a less than proportionate depressing effect on employment.

Railway profits, on the other hand, increase and decrease out of proportion to traffic and revenues. In the United States, during the good years of the interwar period, the railroad companies used large portions of their profits to finance improvements in plant and equipment. Presumably the manner in which investment is financed has something to do with its impact on the national economy. British railways appropriated virtually all earnings for payments to security holders (Table 38). Their rather modest capital expenditures were financed from other sources than earnings.

The British railway companies did, however, follow a system of operating expenditure that was potentially countercyclical. In some years they spent more, especially for maintenance, than they charged against current revenue, charging the balance to "renewal" or "suspense" accounts. In other years they charged greater sums against revenue than they actually spent. The countercyclical effect was not very regular in practice. The maximum excess of total expenditure over the sum regarded as attributable to the current volume of traffic did not always occur in a trough year. The minimum excess, or the maximum postponement of expenditure, did not always occur in a peak year. In any case, the amounts involved were small.

While some analysts of cycles have occupied themselves with the effect of investment on sales, others have concerned themselves with the effect of sales on investment. In particular, it has been supposed that an increase in the physical volume of business necessitates an increase in the stock of equipment used to handle that business. Applied to periods no longer than a business expansion, this idea finds little support in railway operating experience. British railways handle considerable increases in their traffic largely by keeping their equipment in use more of the time. Stocks of equipment sometimes diminished during an expansion of traffic. Over longer periods the idea has more validity. The tremendous cumulative growth of traffic during the nineteenth and early twentieth centuries could not have been cared for without a great accumulation of equipment. Since 1920 increases in traffic during business expansions have been almost offset or more than offset by decreases during contractions, and stocks of equipment have also increased very little or have gradually declined.

Business men increase or diminish their current investment expendi-

TABLE 38

Net Revenue, Interest and Dividends; and "Excess" Expenditure, 1919-1938
(absolute figures in millions of pounds)

					PER CENT OF NET REVENUE		
			INTEREST AND DIVIDENDS		*Appropriated*	*Paid*	EXCESS OF
YEAR	LEVEL OF BUSINESS	NET REVENUE	*Appropriated*	Paid[a]	$(2)\div(1)$ $\times 100$	$(3)\div(1)$ $\times 100$	EXPENDITURE[b]
		(1)	(2)	(3)	(4)	(5)	(6)
1919	Trough	49.5	48.3	......	97.6	......	−.9
1920	Peak	49.4	48.2	48.4	97.6	98.0	−1.3
1921	Trough	44.0	48.4	47.9	110.0	108.9	.5
1922		51.3	52.0	52.4	101.4	102.1	−5.1
1923		49.3	50.0	49.9	101.4	101.2	−.1
1924	Peak	44.9	50.1	49.9	111.6	111.1	2.5
1925		42.3	49.3	49.2	116.5	116.3	6.6
1926	Trough	24.0	42.0	41.9	175.0	174.6	3.6
1927	Peak	46.7	46.4	46.4	99.4	99.4	2.3
1928	Trough	45.2	44.9	44.9	99.3	99.3	2.5
1929	Peak	49.3	48.4	48.3	98.2	98.0	1.2
1930		42.0	43.8	43.8	104.3	104.3	2.4
1931		37.6	38.4	38.5	102.1	102.4	1.9
1932	Trough	30.4	31.9	31.7	104.9	104.3	.5
1932	Trough	27.2	28.8	28.7	105.9	105.5	.7
1933		29.6	30.8	30.7	104.1	103.7	−1.5
1934		32.3	33.1	33.0	102.5	102.2	1.2
1935		33.7	34.3	34.3	101.8	101.8	4.3
1936		36.5	36.4	36.5	99.7	100.0	4.5
1937	Peak	38.7	38.2	38.3	98.7	99.0	1.6
1938	Trough	29.8	29.9	30.1	100.3	101.0	1.1

[a] Amount appropriated, plus any decrease or minus any increase in the balance sheet accounts, "Unpaid interest and dividends" and "Interest and dividends payable or accruing and provided for."

[b] Excess of operating expenditures made over operating expenditures charged against gross receipts of the year, in the income account. A negative figure means that expenditures made were less than expenditures charged against receipts. Outlays on other operations as well as railway operations were included in computing these figures.

tures from time to time for reasons other than the current level of their sales or the recent direction of change in sales. Consumers likewise vary their expenditures for reasons other than the recent level or trend of their incomes. To a large extent these other reasons center around the emergence, improvement, cheapening, and growing availability of new objects of expenditure, especially those of a durable character. It is a safe bet, for example, that more people with incomes of about $4000 bought television sets in 1949 than in 1948. When the motives for increasing expenditure prevail over these for diminishing it, business at large is likely to expand; when the predominance is the other way around, it is likely to contract. In the nineteenth century, developments in transport opened vast new prospects of expenditure. Promoters and investors saw prospects of profits from building railroads. Merchants and manufacturers visualized a means of broadening their markets. Consumers found travel more inviting. In our own century, motor transport has largely taken over the role formerly played by the railroads.

When depressive influences preponderate over stimulating influences, many of the latter may nevertheless continue to operate and, when reinforced by new impulses, may help turn the tide again. Such influences can sometimes be identified from the cyclical pattern of the data. When consumers rapidly increase their outlays on a particular object of expenditure during business expansion, and diminish their outlays very little or not at all during business contraction, one may fairly infer that the "propensity" to spend for that object is rising. The propensity for motoring rose in Britain throughout the interwar period; the number of cars in use increased in every contraction. (The propensity for motor-cycling declined, at least after 1927.) On the business side, the number of motor trucks registered likewise increased continuously. These influences show themselves also in the consumption of motor fuel, the annual supply of which increased from year to year in every interwar contraction, except for a slight dip from 1924 to 1925 and from 1930 to 1931.

When the British government entered the war, it provided an obvious instance of an increase in spending prompted by something other than an increase in the receipts of the spender. In an industrially powerful and uninvaded country, war has many effects like those of other economic stimulants. Large quantities of goods and large numbers of men had to be moved; there was an unusually great boom in railway traffic. Centralized control of transport facilities and routing, and the tolerance of congestion on passenger trains, accentuated the railroads' usual ability to handle growing traffic without proportionate expansion of employment or stocks of equipment. The conveyance of durable goods and of materials for making them doubtless increased faster than other freight traffic. The final uses, naturally, were different — war construction and munitions; we have seen how the railroads themselves had to curtail ordinary maintenance.

Peace brought a new kind of stimulus. There was a rush to buy long unavailable durable goods, and to resume other expenditures that had been discouraged. The railways endeavored to make up for neglected maintenance.[1] Owners of motor vehicles quickly restored them to circulation, booming the market for commodities associated with their use. Such impulses of reconversion must eventually fade, of course; future business expansion must depend on other and perhaps less readily identifiable stimulants.

[1] This was difficult. As late as 1949 we find the Railway Executive complaining that "the shortage of materials . . . governs the rate at which arrears of renewals can be overtaken."

Note on Sources of Information

Except as noted elsewhere in this paper, all figures and other factual material used have been taken from the sources described in this note.

Whenever quarterly or monthly figures of any kind, in their original form, suggest the presence of seasonal influences, the data presented in the paper have been computed by seasonally adjusting the original figures.

Railway Data in General

Official sources

All data for 1913 and earlier were taken from the Parliamentary Papers listed in Table 39. With four exceptions they were issued by the Board of Trade or one of its component units. Titles are too long, cumbrous, and variable to cite in detail. For this period only, Ireland is included.

For 1919 and later periods most data are from various issues of serial publications by the Ministry of Transport. Annual data: 1919-38 from *Railway Returns. Returns of the Capital, Traffic, Receipts and Working Expenditure, etc., of the Railway Companies of Great Britain . . .* ; 1939-47 from *Summary Table of Statistical Returns of Railways of Great Britain, 1938 to 1944,* and same, *1945, 1946, 1947;* financial data, 1940-47 from the annual publication, *Government Control of Railways.* Monthly and four-weekly data: 1920-39 from *Railway Statistics.*

We have obtained some further railway data for 1939 and later years from Central Statistical Office, *Annual Abstract of Statistics* and *Monthly Digest of Statistics.*

Detailed annual data for the nationalized part of the transport industry appear in the British Transport Commission's *Reports and Accounts.* For 1951, the Commission issued two documents, a general discussion in its *Report* and detailed figures in its *Financial and Statistical Accounts.* Monthly or four-weekly data appear in its *Transport Statistics* (first issue, January 1948).

Comparability from year to year

The summary figures for all railways in *Railway Returns* are presented on two bases: 1919-32, including the railways transferred to the London Passenger Transport Board in 1933; 1928-38, excluding those railways. (Figures on the latter basis were published retroactively for 1928-32.)

For passenger traffic only, the *Returns* also present figures for 1919-27 excluding the London tubes and the Metropolitan District railway. To make these figures comparable with those for 1928-38, the traffic of the Metropolitan (not to be confused with the Metropolitan *District*) must be deducted, and that of the Whitechapel & Bow Joint line added. In preparing the data for Charts 8 and 11, we made these adjustments.

A new accounting system was introduced on January 1, 1928. Comparable figures were published retroactively for 1927 but no earlier years.

Wherever there is a break at 1927 in our tables and charts, the earlier segment is based on the old and the later on the new accounting system. Wherever there is a break at 1928 or 1932, the earlier segment includes the London underground lines and the later segment does not include them.

The change in accounting system or railway basis does not always change the figures. The new and the old accounting systems sometimes produce the same figure for 1927. LPTB had practically no freight; hence items pertaining to freight traffic, service, and equipment may not be affected. In such instances the three segments become two, or even one.

Monthly and quarterly estimates

Except for passenger traffic, the data in *Railway Statistics, Monthly Digest of Statistics,* and *Transport Statistics* pertain to four-week periods, beginning in 1932; 13 sets of data are published each year. We estimated monthly ton-miles by apportioning those reported for each four-week period according to the number of days in that period that fell in each month. For example, we estimated April 1934 as follows:

Period	Ton-Miles in Period (millions) (1)	April Days in Period (2)	Ton-miles in April Formula (3)	Amount (millions) (4)
4 weeks ended April 21	1,218	21	21/28×(1)	914
4 weeks ended May 19	1,212	9	9/28×(1)	390
April	....	....	Sum of (4)	1,304

We found, however, that it would be too laborious to prepare monthly estimates on this plan for the numerous measures of railway operations, such as wagon-miles, train-miles, train-hours, and contented ourselves with quarterly estimates, made with the help of the ratios in Table 40. For example, coaching trains ran 92.09 million miles in the 16 weeks (112 days) ended October 8, 1932. We therefore estimate coaching train miles in the quarter ended September 30, 1932 to have been .815 × 92.09 or 75.05 million. Figures produced in this way were seasonally adjusted and finally divided by 3 to make them comparable with monthly data for earlier years.

In computing averages during, rather than aggregates for, a quarter, we simply

TABLE 39

Sources of Data for 1913 and Prior Years

References are to Accounts and Papers Published for Houses of Parliament[a]

SESSIONAL YEAR	VOLUME NUMBER	PAPER NUMBER	SESSIONAL YEAR	VOLUME NUMBER	PAPER NUMBER
1847-48	XXVI[b]	938[c]	1863	LXII	492
1850	LIII	10[c]	1865	XLIX	456
1851	LI	12[c]	1867	LXII	516
1851	LI	313[c]	1868-69	LIV	286
1852-53	XCVII	252	1870	LIX	c. 229
1852-53	XCVII	906	1875	LXVII	c. 1332
1854	LXII	1844	1882	LX	c. 3329
1854-55	XLVIII	1932	1885	LVIII	c. 4819
1856	LIV	2147	1890	LXV	c. 6157
1857[d]	XXXVII	2258	1899	LXXXV	c. 9457
1859	XXV	2472	1903	LXXVI	cd. 4804
1859	XXV	2513	1913	LX	cd. 8038
1861	LVII	2871			

[a] Sometimes referred to as "Parliamentary Papers" or "Sessional Papers."
[b] Entitled "Reports of Commissioners" rather than "Accounts and Papers."
[c] These reports were made by the Office of Commissioners of Railways. All others were made by the Board of Trade or a department thereof.
[d] Second Session.

took a straight average of the four-week figures. Thus the number of steam locomotives in stock during the four-week periods ending July 16, August 13, September 10, and October 8, 1932 was 22,189, 22,154, 22,109, and 22,061 respectively. The average of these figures is 22,128, which we take to be the average during the quarter ended September 30, 1932.

In addition to the monthly estimates of ton-miles we made quarterly estimates

TABLE 40

Estimation of Quarterly from Four-Weekly Data

QUARTER TO BE ESTIMATED (1)	PERIOD TO WHICH DATA USED AS BASIS OF ESTIMATE PERTAIN		RATIO OF DAYS IN QUARTER TO DAYS IN BASIS PERIOD, 91.25 ÷ (3) (4)
	Ending date[a] (2)	*No. of days included* (3)	
First	March 18-27	84	1.086
Second	June 10-19	84	1.086
Third	Sept. 30-Oct. 9	112	.815
Fourth	Dec. 23-Jan. 1	84	1.086

[a] Varies from year to year over range indicated.

by the same method as for operating aggregates, so as to have ton-miles comparable with the operating data. The trough in monthly ton-miles came in December 1932, but the trough in quarterly ton-miles came in the second quarter of 1933. The monthly 1937 peak, June, falls within the peak quarter, i.e. the second quarter of the year, and the monthly 1938 trough within the quarterly trough, i.e. the third quarter. In marking off cycles on charts of operating data we use the quarterly chronology in years for which our data are quarterly.

Supply of Commodities

Particulars of the tonnage of each of certain "selected traffics" originated by the railways, 1928-38, are contained in *Railway Returns*. We determined the commodities included in each traffic category by consulting *Railway Statistics* (which contains descriptive notes and more detailed figures) and the *General Classification of Merchandise,* January 1938 edition, published by the Railway Clearing House, London. We then attempted to compile figures on the total annual supply of the commodities in each group. Ideally such a figure should not only include production and imports of all the articles, and no others, but should be adjusted for changes in stocks at point of origin. No such adjustment was possible, however, and even the production and import data leave something to be desired.[1] Our supply estimates appear in Table 4, and changes in them are compared with changes in the aggregate tonnage of the corresponding selected traffics in Table 5. In the tables we assign each commodity group a number. The corresponding traffic descriptions, and the derivation of our figures on supply, are indicated in the following paragraphs.

1. *Creosote, tar, and pitch.* Production and imports of creosote not included in any year; no data 1928-30. Domestic production of creosote was from 13.3 to 19.5 per cent of total supply shown here, 1931-38. Imports include both coal tar and pitch and "other sorts."

2. *Grain, flour, and milling offals.* Production of barley, beans, oats, peas, rye, wheat. (The railway classification indicates that beans and peas are covered by the traffic category.) Any beans, peas, or rye grown in Scotland not included. No data on output of mill products. Total imports of grain and flour, as classified in the import statistics, minus: macaroni, spaghetti and vermicelli; maize starch for use as food; and farinaceous substances for use as food, all of which are separately rated in the railway classification. Also imports of cereal by-products as totaled in the import statistics, and of seeds for expressing oils. Original import data in cwt. (112 lbs.) converted to long tons by dividing by 20.

3. *Gravel and sand.* Production less quantities for road-making and ballast. The merchandise classification provides that gravel for roads shall be classified as

---

[1] Because of the paucity of industrial statistics we were unable to prepare supply figures for 6 of the 19 "selected traffics." For similar reasons we have done nothing with any of the somewhat different commodity groups for which commodity statistics were published, 1921-27.

106

road-making and road-repairing material. It does not specifically provide for sand for roads but we assume such sand would be so rated. Gravel and sand for ballast are presumably used by railroads and not comparable with revenue traffic.

4. *Iron ore.* Production including and imports excluding manganiferous ore.

5. *Iron and steel blooms, billets, and ingots.* Production of steel ingots (converter acid and basic, open hearth acid and basic, and electric). Imports of steel blooms, billets and slabs, and ingots. Special steels not included in either production or imports.

6. *Iron and steel, other descriptions.* The supply of materials is assumed to indicate roughly the flow of products. Supply as for No. 5, plus production of steel castings (electric and all other) and imports of: steel bars, rods, angles, shapes and sections; plates and sheets; other iron and steel.

7. *Limestone and chalk.* Production of limestone, less quantities for road-making and ballast. Comment on sand for roads, and on ballast under No. 3, applies. Total production of chalk.

8. *Oil cake.* Estimated from imports of oil seeds (except desiccated and flaked coconut intended for food). *Final Report on the Fifth Census of Production,* Part III, p. 364, shows for each kind of seed the quantity crushed and the output of cake and meal in 1934 and 1935. We computed ratios of output to input, averaged them for the two years, and applied them to inputs. The factors are .326 for coconuts, .664 for cottonseed, .678 for flaxseed, .307 for ground nuts (peanuts etc.), .469 for palm kernel, .616 for rapeseed, and .700 for soya beans. (Imports of undecorticated ground nuts were multiplied by .67 to give the decorticated equivalent, which was then added to decorticated imports before applying the .307 factor.) Imports in the form of seed and meal added to these production estimates.

9. *Pig iron.* Production (excluding ferro-alloys). Imports.

10. *Road-making and road-repairing material.* Production of igneous rocks, gravel and sand, limestone, and sandstone for road-making and ballasting, less ballast used by railroads (latter from *Railway Returns*). Ballast converted from cubic yards to tons by dividing by 1.21, a ratio confidentially furnished by a large American railroad.

11. *Timber.* No production data available. Annual production is estimated to be roughly 50 million cubic feet or about 1 million tons (W. F. Hiley, *The Economics of Forestry* (Clarendon Press, 1930), p. 51; Interdepartmental Home-Grown Timber Committee of the Forestry Commission, *Interim Report,* 1933, Appendix II, p. 10), less than one-seventh of the supply (imports) shown here. Imports of hewn, sawn (not further prepared) and planed or dressed timber, plus those of pitprops and other pitwood. Original data converted to tons on basis of following ratios: Hewn and sawn oak, 40 cubic feet. Mahogany, teak, persimmon, hickory, cornel and unspecified hardwoods, 45 cubic feet. Walnut, 50 cubic feet. Planed or dressed hardwoods, all softwoods, also pitprops and other pitwood, 1.32 loads per ton. Exceptions, 1936-38: hewn fir, pine, spruce, etc., and pitprops, 0.55 fathoms per ton; other hewn softwoods, all sawn softwoods, planed or dressed softwoods, 0.4 standards per ton; planed or dressed hardwoods, 45 cubic feet per

107

ton; other pitwood reported in tons. Conversion factors from *Annual Statement of the Trade of the United Kingdom*, Vol. I, 1938.

12. *Potatoes.* Production, imports.

13. *Vegetables, other than potatoes.* Production of carrots (except in Scotland), marigolds, onions (except in Scotland), sugar beets, turnips and swedes. Imports of onions, converted from cwt. by dividing by 20.

Production data are from various annual issues of: Imperial Institute, Mineral Resources Dept., *The Mineral Industry of the British Empire and Foreign Countries* (creosote, tar and pitch, iron ore); Ministry of Agriculture and Fisheries, *Agricultural Statistics* (grain, potatoes, other vegetables); Secretary of Mines, *Annual Report* (gravel and sand, limestone and chalk, road-making and road-repairing materials); National Federation of Iron and Steel Manufacturers, *Statistics of the Iron and Steel Industries* (Iron and steel,[2] pig iron[2]). Import data are from Board of Trade, *Statistical Abstract for the United Kingdom*, or Customs and Excise Dept., *Annual Statement of the Trade of the United Kingdom with British and Foreign Countries*, Vol. I.

[2] 1938 figures from *Statistical Abstract*.

List of Tables

110

List of Charts

111

112

BOOKS

Migration and Business Cycles (1926) Harry Jerome	258 pp., $2.50
Business Cycles: The Problem and Its Setting (1927) Wesley C. Mitchell	514 pp., 5.00
Strategic Factors in Business Cycles (1934) John Maurice Clark	256 pp., *
German Business Cycles, 1924-1933 (1934) Carl T. Schmidt	308 pp., 2.50
Public Works in Prosperity and Depression (1935) Arthur D. Gayer	482 pp., 3.00
Prices in Recession and Recovery (1936) Frederick C. Mills	602 pp., 4.00
Some Theoretical Problems Suggested by the Movements of Interest Rate, Bond Yields and Stock Prices in the United States since 1856 (1938) Frederick R. Macaulay	612 pp., 5.00
Measuring Business Cycles (1946) Arthur F. Burns and Wesley C. Mitchell	592 pp., 5.00
American Transportation in Prosperity and Depression (1948) Thor Hultgren	432 pp., 5.00
Inventories and Business Cycles, with Special Reference to Manufacturers' Inventories (1950) Moses Abramovitz	672 pp., 6.00
Deterioration in the Quality of Foreign Bonds Issued in the United States, 1920-1930 (1951) Ilse Mintz	112 pp., 2.00
What Happens during Business Cycles: A Progress Report (1951) Wesley C. Mitchell	422 pp., 5.00
Conference on Business Cycles (1951) Universities-National Bureau Committee for Economic Research	448 pp., 6.00
Federal Grants and the Business Cycle (1952) James A. Maxwell	136 pp., 2.00
Regularization of Business Investment (1954) Universities-National Bureau Committee for Economic Research	512 pp., 8.00
Frontiers of Economic Knowledge (1954) Arthur F. Burns	410 pp., 5.00

*Available from Augustus M. Kelley, Inc., 31 East 10th Street, New York 3, N. Y.

PAPERS

Railway Freight Traffic in Prosperity and Depression (Occasional
Paper 5, 1942) $ .25
Thor Hultgren

Railroad Travel and the State of Business (Occasional Paper 13, 1943)   .35
Thor Hultgren

Railway Traffic Expansion and Use of Resources in World War II
(Occasional Paper 15, 1944)   .35
Thor Hultgren

The Structure of Postwar Prices (Occasional Paper 27, 1948)   .75
Frederick C. Mills

Wesley Mitchell and the National Bureau (Twenty-ninth Annual Report,
May 1949)   gratis
Arthur F. Burns

Statistical Indicators of Cyclical Revivals and Recessions (Occasional
Paper 31, 1950)   1.50
Geoffrey H. Moore

Cyclical Diversities in the Fortunes of Industrial Corporations
(Occasional Paper 32, 1950)   .50
Thor Hultgren

Behavior of Wage Rates during Business Cycles (Occasional Paper 34, 1950)   1.00
Daniel Creamer

New Facts on Business Cycles (Thirtieth Annual Report, May 1950)   gratis
Arthur F. Burns

Trends and Cycles in Corporate Bond Financing (Occasional Paper 37, 1952)   .75
W. Braddock Hickman

Business Cycle Research and the Needs of Our Times (Thirty-third
Annual Report, May 1953)   gratis
Arthur F. Burns

Transport and the State of Trade in Britain (Occasional Paper 40, 1953)   1.50
Thor Hultgren

*Trends and Cycles in Capital Formation by United States Railroads,
1870-1950* (Occasional Paper)   (in press)
Melville J. Ulmer

114

How to Obtain
National Bureau Publications

The National Bureau of Economic Research is a nonprofit membership corporation organized to make impartial studies in economic science.

Its books are published and distributed (since April 1, 1953) by Princeton University Press; its *Occasional Papers* and *Technical Papers* are published and distributed by the National Bureau itself.

Publications may be obtained either on contributing subscriptions or by purchase.

A contributor of $25 or more a year receives a complimentary copy of each current publication — *books, Occasional Papers, Technical Papers,* and the *Annual Report* — in advance of release to the public. In addition, a contributor is entitled to a one-third discount on all National Bureau publications purchased.

An associate contributor of $5 a year receives complimentary copies of *Occasional Papers, Technical Papers,* and the *Annual Report,* and is entitled to a one-third discount on all publications purchased. Only the following are eligible to become associates: teachers, students, and libraries in recognized educational institutions; members of scientific societies or of private nonprofit research agencies.

A contributor of $2 receives four issues of the *Occasional Paper* or *Technical Paper,* and the *Annual Report.*

Contributions to the National Bureau are deductible in calculating federal income taxes.

NON-CONTRIBUTORS should send orders for *books* to:

Princeton University Press
Princeton, New Jersey

NON-CONTRIBUTORS should send orders for *Papers* and requests for the *Annual Report* directly to:	**CONTRIBUTORS** should send all orders for *books* and *Papers,* and requests for the *Annual Report* directly to:

NATIONAL BUREAU OF ECONOMIC RESEARCH, INC.
1819 Broadway   New York 23, N. Y.

Capital and Output

Trends in Manufacturing

Industries, 1880-1948

DANIEL CREAMER

Assisted by

MARTIN BERNSTEIN

STUDIES IN CAPITAL FORMATION AND FINANCING

OCCASIONAL PAPER 41

NATIONAL BUREAU OF ECONOMIC RESEARCH, INC.